Pablo Casals

Cellist of Conscience

by Jim Hargrove

 CHILDRENS PRESS®
CHICAGO

ACKNOWLEDGMENTS

The editors would like to acknowledge use of excerpted material from the following works:

From "Catalonia: Spain's Country Within a Country" by Randall Peffer. Printed in *National Geographic* magazine. January 1984.

JOYS AND SORROWS: Reflections by Pablo Casals by Albert E. Kahn. © copyright 1970 by Albert E. Kahn. Reprinted by permission of Simon & Schuster, Inc.

From CONVERSATIONS WITH CASALS by J. Ma. Corredor. Translated by Andre Mangeot. Copyright © 1965 by E.P. Dutton. Reprinted by permission of the publisher, Dutton, an imprint of New American Library, a division of Penguin Books USA Inc. Published with permission of Century Hutchinson Publishing, Ltd., London, England.

From PABLO CASALS: A BIOGRAPHY by H.L. Kirk. Copyright © 1974 by H.L. Kirk. Published by Holt, Rinehart and Winston, Inc. Used by permission of Brandt & Brandt, Literary Agents, Inc.

Reprinted from PABLO CASALS by Lillian Littlehales, copyright 1929, copyright renewed 1957; revised and enlarged edition 1948, copyright renewed 1976. Used by permission of W.W. Norton & Company, Inc.

PICTURE ACKNOWLEDGMENTS

AP/Wide World Photos—pages 8, 20, 65 (bottom), 66 (top), 71 (top), 115

The Bettmann Archive—pages 64 (top), 67 (bottom 2 photos), 68 (top), 69 (bottom)

Black Star—© Peter Moeschlin, 65 (top); © Judson Hall, 69 (top); © Paul Senn, 84

Culver Pictures—Frontispiece, page 64 (bottom)

Historical Pictures Service, Chicago—page 67 (top)

United Nations—pages 71 (bottom), 72

UPI/Bettmann Newsphotos—pages 66 (bottom), 68 (bottom), 70 (2 photos)

Cover illustration by Len W. Meents

Library of Congress Cataloging-in-Publication Data

Hargrove, Jim.
    Pablo Casals : cellist of conscience / by Jim Hargrove.
        p.   cm. — (People of distinction)
    Includes bibliographical references and index.
    Summary: Traces the career of the distinguished cellist, including his early years in Spain and the musical accomplishments of his long life.
    ISBN 0-516-03272-0
    1. Casals, Pablo, 1876-1973—Juvenile literature. 2. Violoncellists—Biography—Juvenile literature. [1. Casals, Pablo, 1876-1973. 2. Musicians.] I. Title. II. Series.
ML3930.C265H4   1991
787.4′092—dc20
[B]
                                                    90-21047
                                                         CIP
                                                      MN AC

Table of Contents

Chapter 1

THE CASALS OF CATALONIA

In the northeast corner of Spain, along the shore of the Mediterranean Sea, there is a land called Catalonia. Its history dates back before the time of Jesus. For a brief era during the Middle Ages, it was one of the world's great powers.

Today, Catalonia is a part of the nation of Spain. But it is really a kind of country within a country. Catalans, the people who have lived in Catalonia for a lifetime, have their own language, their own government, and their own flag. In front of government offices and public buildings, the flag of Catalonia often flies next to the flag of Spain.

Modern visitors to this ancient region, little more than half the size of West Virginia, have much to see. Catalonia is a rugged land extending from the Mediterranean Sea to the Pyrenees mountains.

The city of Barcelona is in the heart of Catalonia along the Mediterranean coast. This bustling seaport with nearly two million inhabitants is Spain's most important industrial center.

Away from the larger cities, country roads lead travelers past lovely vineyards and farmlands. Here, modern trucks and automobiles sometimes have to slow down to pass wooden carts pulled by donkeys. Many roads lead to the hills, where ancient villages and historic church buildings are nestled between craggy mountain peaks.

The people of Catalonia, even more than the land, give the region a special charm. Modern visitors may still be lucky enough to see one of the area's amazing old traditions. On special occasions, Catalan men and boys play together in a remarkable way. Standing on each other's shoulders, they form human pyramids. The strongest men stand at the bottom while the smallest boys climb to the top. A successful pyramid can reach the combined height of seven people, towering over the rooftops of three-story buildings.

The Catalan tradition of building human pyramids is centuries old. From a very early age many Catalan boys, including one named Pablo Casals, practiced for the feat by standing on a relative's shoulders. In the Catalan language, these towering formations have various names, including *Castells* "castle towers" and *Xiquet de Vals* "human pyramids."

Another Catalan word, more difficult to translate, is *seny*. A woman from Barcelona once explained its meaning to a magazine writer. "Seny is a Catalan word," she said. "It describes a trait usual in Catalans. When persons have seny, they are proper; they know what they want, have good sense; some people think they are driven."[1] One Catalan who had plenty of seny was Pablo Casals.

Until his death on October 22, 1973, Pablo Casals was known as the finest player of the violoncello on earth. The violoncello is a large stringed musical instrument more commonly called the cello. At an early age, Pablo Casals developed a revolutionary technique for playing the cello, one that is followed by most other cellists to this day. He also became well known as a composer of music and, even more so, as a symphony orchestra conductor.

He lived for nearly a century. During most of his long life, his music was known throughout the world. In 1894, at the age of seventeen, he earned a music scholarship from the queen of Spain. Five years later, in 1899, he played a concert for England's Queen Victoria. Five years after that, during his 1904 tour of the United States he played for President Theodore Roosevelt in the White House.

More than half a century later, in 1961, he gave another performance at the White House, this time for President John F. Kennedy. Even after all those years, his remarkable career was far from over. A full decade later he was still delighting audiences conducting orchestras at the Marlboro Music Festival in Vermont and elsewhere.

But the music of Pablo Casals is only part of the story of his life. In a sense, he became as well known for refusing to play his cello in public as for his legendary performances. He was forced to leave his native country when a military dictator took control there shortly before World War II. For decades he refused to play the cello in public in any nation that recognized the government of Spain.

He was both a musician and a soldier, although he often noted that music was his only weapon. With a bow, a cello, and a conductor's baton, he helped to change the world.

Pablo Casals was born on Friday afternoon, December 29, 1876, in a Catalan town called Vendrell. Located about forty-four miles southwest of Barcelona, the town had about four thousand residents at the time of his birth.

Pablo almost died the same day he was born. A midwife saved him from strangulation by carefully loosening the umbilical cord wrapped around his neck. His birth was recorded two days later using the Spanish name Pablo. In the Catalan language, however, his name was *Pau*, a word meaning "peace."

Even as late as 1876, many children throughout the world died at birth or during the first few years of life. In all, Pablo's mother gave birth to eleven children. Seven of the first eight died as babies or children or during young adulthood. Only Pablo lived a normal lifetime. Within a few years of his birth, a medical miracle was needed to keep him alive as well.

Pablo's mother, born Pilar Ursula Defilló y Amiguet, came to Vendrell in the early 1870s from her home in Puerto Rico. Her father, a critic of Spanish rule in Puerto Rico, had been hounded to death by the Spanish government while his daughter was still in her teens. Pilar's mother and father had moved to Puerto Rico from Barcelona in the 1840s. Both came from old and distinguished Catalan families.

Pablo's father, Carlos Casals, belonged to a family of papermakers that had lived in Spanish Catalonia for centuries. Carlos did not take part in the papermaking business of his relatives, however. Instead, he worked as a piano teacher and as the organist and choir director in a Vendrell church. He was a skilled musician, admired throughout the city.

Although Vendrell was a short distance north of the Mediterranean Sea, Pablo Casals's earliest memories were of time spent along the seacoast. About two and a half miles south of Vendrell was a little seacoast village called San Salvador. In the village was a large home with little rooms that could be rented inexpensively.

"When I was less than a year old, my mother began taking me to the nearby seaside hamlet of San Salvador," Pablo said in a book about his life. "She took me there, she later told me, for the sea air. There was a small church at San Salvador that we would visit. . . . Light sifted through the windows, and the only sound was the whisper of the sea. . . . As I grew older, I would remain for hours gazing from those windows at the sea, marveling at how it stretched endlessly away, and how the waves marched tirelessly to the shore and the clouds formed changing patterns in the sky. It was a sight that never ceased to enthrall me."[2]

Although they were members of an old and distinguished family, Carlos and Pilar Casals were poor. Pablo was lucky that his mother was able to bring him to San Salvador. As Pablo himself explained, it "was the only luxury we could afford, as our family had very modest means and expenses had to be calculated carefully."[3]

The sound of wind rustling leaves drifted through the steady rhythm of the Mediterranean Sea in Pablo's earliest memories. But his ear soon turned to music—especially to his family piano.

"I remember when I was two or three," Pablo said, "sitting on the floor and resting my head against the piano to hear better what my father was playing. I was transported. I also remember that when my brother Artur and I were very young, my father ordered us to stand behind the piano. . . . We had to name the notes of anything he played at random."[4]

Pablo once said that he learned to sing before he could speak. For him musical notes were as familiar as words. With his father as his teacher, he began to study the piano at the age of four.

He became a professional musician at five. On April 27, 1882, he began singing in the second-soprano section of the

Vendrell church choir. The choir was directed by his father. His mother added a few coins to the tiny payment he received for singing during each mass. "I was paid for every service," he recalled, "my fee amounted to the sum of ten cents; and so one might say that this was my first professional job as a musician."[5]

The first year he joined the church choir, he was thrilled to be able to sing in a dawn Christmas mass. "I hardly slept the night before," he said, "and it was pitch-black when my father came into my room to tell me it was time to get ready to go to the services. When we stepped out of the house it was dark and cold—so cold that bundled up as I was, the chill went right through my clothes and I shivered as we walked, though I did not shiver only because of the cold. It was all so mysterious; I felt that something wonderful was about to happen. High overhead the heavens were still full of stars, and as we walked in silence I held my father's hand, feeling he was my protector and guide. The village was hushed, and in the dark narrow streets there were moving figures, shadowy and spectral and silent too, moving toward the church in the starry night. Then, suddenly, there was a burst of light—flooding from the open doors of the church. We moved into that light and into the church, silently, with the other people. My father played the organ, and when I sang, it was my heart that was singing and I poured out everything that was in me."[6]

Even as a young child, Pablo developed a sense of wonder about music that would last a lifetime. In just a few years, the fascination extended from singing to experiments with a variety of musical instruments. Under his father's instruction, he continued his study of the piano. As soon as his son's developing technique permitted it, Carlos introduced him to the simpler piano pieces of Beethoven, Mendelssohn, Chopin, and Bach.

During his sixth year, Pablo began going to school, but his interest in music and musical instruments kept growing. He began playing a little piccolo, actually a simple penny whistle, that he found in the house. When he tried to play it in a parade, however, he fainted. His father, on the advice of a doctor, took away the toy. Actually, the doctor's warning was just the excuse Carlos wanted. He disapproved of his young son learning to play an instrument of little musical value.

During the same year, three musicians visited the Casals home. The musicians asked Carlos to teach them a new dance, hoping to play the tune on a Catalan folk instrument called a *gralla*. Sounding a bit like an oboe, the gralla was difficult to play. Neverthless, six-year-old Pablo learned to play the new tune on one in just a few minutes.

By his seventh year, Pablo's gift for playing music became even more obvious. He had already learned a skill that many adult musicians find difficult. The youngster could transpose any melody into a different key. In other words, he could begin a tune on a slightly higher or lower note that was different from the original key. By doing so, it was necessary to change every note in the melody, often adding sharps or flats to many different tones. He could play transposed tunes on the piano, and write them down on paper as well. He even helped his father by composing and writing down some original melodies to be played in Vendrell's Catholic church. One of his original manuscripts, from Christmas 1883, still exists.

At the same time, he began to study the violin, the most well known of all the orchestral stringed instruments. To his surprise, many of the other schoolchildren in Vendrell made fun of him. Some said that he looked like a blind man as he played. "What could you expect," Pablo said many years later, "when the only violinists they had seen were blind beggars in cafés and the streets?"[7]

Of all the musical instruments he saw and heard, Pablo most wanted to learn to play the organ. Huge organs like the one his father performed upon in the Vendrell church could produce a larger range of notes, with more tonal shades, than any other instrument. The fingers of both hands were used to play the organ's keys. Even the feet were needed to push the pedals beneath the huge keyboard. Although he was an expert organist, Carlos was unwilling to teach his son how to play the organ.

"I longed especially to play the organ," Pablo remembered. "But my father said I could not touch the instrument until my feet could reach the pedals. How I waited for that day! I was never very tall, so the day took somewhat longer to arrive than it would have for another child."[8]

As an adult, wearing shoes, Pablo Casals stood less than five feet three inches tall. He was nine years old before his legs grew long enough to reach the pedals on his father's organ. When the great day finally arrived, however, he showed that he was as quick a student of the organ as of other musical instruments. Of course his years of practice at the piano helped greatly.

A year or so before he began playing the organ, the youngster discovered another musical instrument. In 1885, a group of traveling musicians dressed as clowns appeared in a public square in Vendrell.

The performers, who called themselves *Los Tres Bemoles* "The Three Flats," played unusual instruments. Teacups, glasses filled to varying heights with water, spoons, cigar-box guitars, bells, and a washtub drum were some of the instruments used by The Three Flats.

Little Pablo was among the people who crowded around the musicians during one of their strange performances. "I listened spellbound to every note they played," Pablo remembered years later. "I was especially fascinated by their instruments. . . . One man played on a broom handle that was strung something like a cello—though I had never seen or even heard of a cello at that time. For some reason . . . that broom-handle instrument fascinated me most of all."[9]

The boy rushed home to tell his father about the new musical instrument. Carlos laughed as he heard it described. But Pablo continued talking with great excitement. Finally, the father said, "All right, Pablo, I'll make you an instrument like it."[10]

Actually Carlos and a family friend made a much better cello than the one used by The Three Flats. The homemade instrument included a long, slender gourd that made the single string sound louder when it was plucked. By pressing down on the string at various spots, sounds of different pitches—even entire scales—could be played.

Pablo experimented with the gourd cello for just a few minutes. Then he played a tune by Schubert on it! His lifelong love affair with the cello had begun.

Casals began playing on a homemade cello, but later he used a Mateo Goffriller cello made in Venice, Italy, about 1720.

Chapter 2

THE TOST KID

Pablo Casals grew from a boy enchanted by a homemade cello to one of the most famous musicians the world has ever known. But a medical miracle was needed to help him through his tenth year.

In 1887 Pablo was bitten in the leg by a rabid dog who had been wandering the streets of Vendrell for days. Most people thought that there was little hope. Rabies, the dreaded disease spread by the bite of rabid animals, almost always brought death to its victims.

Just two years earlier, in 1885, the French scientist Louis Pasteur for the first time injected a human being with a vaccine that prevented development of the fatal sickness. The following year, the first large-scale tests of his vaccine were made on humans.

By 1887, the year Pablo was bitten, Pasteur's vaccine was hardly out of the experimental stage. Fortunately, the Casals's family physician, Dr. Valls, knew that a hospital in Barcelona was already administering it.

Carlos Casals and his son rushed to catch the next train bound for Barcelona. The father quickly brought Pablo to the hospital there.

Until the 1980s, when treatment was vastly simplified, rabies vaccinations were extremely painful. In Pablo's case, a series of sixty-four injections had to be given—two each day for more than a month. The serum contained in the needles had to be boiling hot to be effective.

Before the first injection was given, Carlos stuffed a handkerchief into Pablo's mouth. "Remember," Carlos told his son, "that men do not cry."[1]

The injections were painful, but Pasteur's miraculous new medicine saved Pablo Casals's life. The very next year, 1888, the eleven-year-old boy found a new purpose that would last throughout his lifetime.

"When I was eleven years old," he said eighty years later, "I heard the cello played for the first time. That was the beginning of a long and cherished companionship! A trio had come to play at a concert in Vendrell—a pianist, a violinist and a cellist. My father took me to the concert."[2] For the first time, Pablo heard a real violoncello played. The cellist was Josep García, a fine player and a professor at Barcelona's Municipal School of Music. In just a few months, Professor García became Pablo's teacher. But from the very beginning, the boy was enchanted by Señor García's beautiful cello.

"When I saw his cello I was fascinated by it—" Pablo remembered, "I had never seen one before. From the moment I heard the first notes I was overwhelmed. I felt as if I could not breathe. There was something so tender, beautiful and human—yes, so very human—about the sound. I had never heard such a beautiful sound before. A radiance filled me. When the first composition was ended, I told my father, 'Father, that is the most wonderful instrument I have ever heard. That is what I want to play.'"[3]

To the eleven-year-old boy, small even for his age, the cello must have seemed like an enormous instrument. Even for an adult, the act of carrying a full-sized cello requires some effort. But Pablo could suddenly think of little else.

At home, he began to hold his little violin in the way a cellist would hold the much larger instrument. Instead of placing it under his chin, as the violin is held, he placed his instrument between his knees. That was the way Professor García held the cello.

When Carlos saw his son mishandling the violin as if it were a cello, he ordered him to stop. But it was clear that Pablo was more interested in the cello than in any other instrument, including the violin and the piano. A few days later, Carlos bought a small cello and gave Pablo a few lessons. Pablo's mother soon noticed that her son seemed to take naturally to the new instrument.

"Pablo shows such enthusiasm for the cello that he must have the chance to study it," Pilar said to her husband. "There is no teacher here in Vendrell who is qualified to teach him properly. We must arrange for him to go to the

School of Music in Barcelona."

"What in the world are you talking about?" Carlos answered in amazement. "How can Pablo possibly go to Barcelona? We simply do not have the money."

Doña Pilar stood her ground. "We will find a way," she said. "I will take him there. Pablo is a musician. This is his nature. This is what he was made to be. He must go anywhere necessary. There is no other choice."[4]

Before long, Pablo's parents began a series of long and bitter arguments about their son's education. From his own life, Carlos knew that it was very difficult to earn a living as a musician. He wanted his son to become a carpenter, and to develop his musical talent as a hobby. In fact, Carlos had already made arrangements for Pablo, on his twelfth birthday, to be apprenticed to a carpenter.

Pilar argued that God had given their son a great talent. She insisted that God would help him find a way to develop it. Pablo would be a musician, she declared, not a carpenter or a shoemaker or anything else.

The arguments flashed for days. "They argued with such bitterness that it pained me terribly and I felt very guilty,"[5] Pablo said. In the end, Carlos finally bowed to his wife's wishes. He wrote to the Barcelona school to find out if his son could be enrolled there.

Barcelona's *Escuela Municipal de Música* (Municipal School of Music) was only two years old when Pablo and his mother arrived there. Pablo performed on the piano and the cello for the school's director, its piano instructors, and the cello professor, Josep García. The officials who heard Pablo play must have been impressed. Pablo was accepted, becoming one of the youngest of the school's four hundred students.

The music school was located in the old section of Barcelona. Many of the buildings there were centuries old. The young student was impressed by the big city's picturesque cafés, its crowded shops and busy seaport, and the spacious parks and museums. Doña Pilar made arrangements for her son to live in the home of Benet and María Boixados, distant relations on her side of the family.

Like most large cities, Barcelona had its share of criminals and street toughs. Benet Boixados, a carpenter by trade, seemed to carry on a solitary battle against the city's outlaws.

"He used to disappear in the evenings," Pablo remembered years later, "apparently to go to the 'dangerous' cafés in the low quarters of Barcelona. His idea was to curb the activities of a lot of toughs he found there. He would come home with knives and pistols he had snatched from them, and kept those trophies in drawers—the only weapon he used was an ash stick! One evening he came home with a wound—he had been knifed! But he just told us it was nothing, and the next evening his comment when he returned, rather pleased with himself, was, 'That chap of yesterday and I are now quits!'"[6]

Benet Boixados's nightly activities were unusual, but Pablo found him to be a kind and generous guardian. A member of the Association for the Protection of Animals and Plants, Benet was as gentle with the young student as he was tough with the city's criminals.

On Pablo's first day at the Municipal School of Music, he was told by one of his teachers to learn a simple passage on the cello. However, the young boy did not understand his homework assignment. He rushed home to the Boixados's house, where his mother was still visiting, and greeted her in tears.

Doña Pilar was certain that her son could do anything asked of him at the school. She suggested that, since he did not understand the instructions, he should write a musical piece based on the notes supplied by the school.

For his first assignment, therefore, Pablo Casals wrote out an original composition for cello. "When I produced it the next day at the class," he said, "my teacher looked at it, seemed to laugh and cry at the same time, and ended by embracing me."[7] The boy had not understood his lesson. At the same time, he had proved that he was a gifted and hardworking student.

In all, Pablo studied at the Municipal School of Music for five years. It was the only formal cello training he ever received. But from his very first weeks at the school, he began doing a remarkable thing.

Throughout much of the world in the late 1800s, when Pablo attended school, there was only one acceptable way to play the cello. The player's right arm, which held the bow, was kept close to the body, the wrist somewhat higher than the elbow. Josep García instructed Pablo and the other students to practice with a small book tucked under the right armpit to learn this unnatural activity. At the same time, movement of the left hand, which held the neck of the cello and pressed down on the appropriate strings at just the right place, was also very restricted.

"I began making certain changes in the then accepted technique of playing the cello," Pablo remembered. "It is true I was only twelve or so at the time, but certain things are obvious even to children. . . . So at home, while I was practicing, I began to devise a method of playing which would free the arms and get rid of that very cramped and artificial position."[8]

In his first year at the music school, Pablo began using his new style in the classroom. When the other students saw how he played, some were outraged. His cello teacher, Josep García, was also startled. However Señor García soon saw the logic behind his student's new approach. "Anyway," Pablo said, "today nobody learns the cello with a book under his armpit!"[9]

A person who learns to play a musical instrument supremely well is sometimes called a *virtuoso*. Of all the virtuosos of the twentieth century, few learned to master an instrument faster than Pablo Casals. After less than a year of study at the Escuela Municipal de Música, he obtained his first job as a professional cellist.

With two other musicians, a pianist and a violinist, he began playing from 9:00 P.M. to midnight seven nights a week at the Café Tost. The café was located on the main street of the town of Gracia, a suburb of Barcelona. His wages of four *pesetas* each night, while low, were not bad for a twelve-year-old boy.

Café musicians were expected to play popular tunes of the day. They were often little waltzes and other dance numbers. The music was generally not as difficult as that written by masters such as Beethoven and Bach. Nevertheless, café audiences approved of listening to the more serious, classical music.

In a matter of weeks, Pablo convinced Señor Tost, owner of the café, to set aside one night each week for classical music. Classical music night became an extremely crowded one at the Café Tost. People even traveled from central Barcelona to hear the trio and, especially, its miraculous little cellist, twelve-year-old Pablo Casals. Before long, he became known as *El Niño del Tost* "The Tost Kid."

During summer vacation after his first year at the music school, Pablo played in a concert in the city of Tarragona, a short distance east of Vendrell. The August 25, 1889 issue of a local newspaper, *La Opinion*, reported on the young cellist: "In individual performance the boy Paulito Casals shone in the violoncello part . . . so much so that we do not hesitate assuring a brilliant future in the study of music if he continues to show today's application and native musical talent."[10]

When summer was over, Pablo returned to the music school and to the Café Tost. Again his playing was extremely popular with audiences at the café. However one part of his young star's behavior bothered the café's owner, Señor Tost.

"I was supposed to be there on the dot of nine o'clock," Pablo remembered. "However, there were exciting things to see in the city, and lots of new ideas for a young boy to think about. I might be strolling down the boulevard of Las Ramblas with its fascinating bird markets and flower stalls, or exploring some neighborhood I'd never seen before, or reading a new book, or just daydreaming in the gardens of the Teatro Lírico; so sometimes I was late to work."[11]

One evening when he arrived late at the café, he found Señor Tost standing in the doorway with a cross expression on his face. The older man reached into his pocket and handed the boy a watch. "All right," he said. "Perhaps this will help teach you the meaning of time."[12]

In a few more years, Pablo Casals was famous throughout the world. At every concert he gave, people knew he would appear on time. His habit of being very punctual was well known.

Chapter 3

A POINT OF HONOR

During the years young Pablo played the cello at the Café Tost, he attracted the attention of many people. One of them was the well-known Catalan composer and pianist Isaac Albéniz. His collection of piano compositions, called *Iberia*, and a number of his orchestral works, including one called *Catalonia*, are still performed occasionally on concert stages today.

As soon as he heard Pablo play, Albéniz became very excited. "You must come with me to London!" he said after the young man's performance. "You must come and work with me there."[1] Pablo was greatly impressed by the offer. But when his mother heard it repeated, she had a different reaction.

"My child is still a child," Pilar said to the noted composer. "He is much too young to go to London and to start traveling around. He must stay here in Barcelona and complete his studies. There will be plenty of time later for other things."

"All right," Albéniz answered, "but your son has a great gift, and I feel I must do whatever I can to help him. Let me give you a letter of introduction to the Count de Morphy in Madrid. He is a wonderful man, a patron of the arts, a splendid musician and brilliant scholar, he is the personal advisor to Queen María Cristina. He has much influence. He can help Pablo's career. When you are ready, take the letter to him."[2]

Doña Pilar held onto the enthusiastic letter from Albéniz for several years. In time, the services of the Count de Morphy would be invaluable. Meanwhile, Pablo continued to develop his skills—and reputation—as a cellist.

After he had played at the Café Tost for several years, the young cellist was offered a better job. At the Café Pajarera (the Spanish word *pajarera* means "bird cage"), he was offered more money and more musicians with whom to play. The café was inside a round building with glass walls. It was the first restaurant in Barcelona to have electric lights, an invention that was rapidly changing the world. At the elegant Pajarera, Pablo and the other musicians played a wider variety of music than the trio at the Café Tost.

Expected to play many more compositions than before, Pablo was always in search of new music to bring to the Café Pajarera. Once a week, his father traveled from Vendrell to spend the day with him. Together, Carlos and his son wandered through the many music stores of Barcelona and the surrounding towns.

During one of his weekly visits, Carlos purchased a full-size cello for his son. Until then, Pablo had been practicing—and performing—on a cello just three-fourths the size of the standard instrument. During the same visit, father and son stopped in an old music store near Barcelona's busy harbor.

Inside the shop, Pablo looked through some dusty piles of old music that had been there for years. Suddenly, he saw some pages that were yellowed with age. The words printed on the paper cover fairly jumped off the page: Six Suites for 'Cello Solo, by Johann Sebastian Bach.

"I wondered what could be hidden there," he remembered, "what mystery lay behind the words: Six Suites for 'Cello Solo. I did not even know they existed, neither did my teacher, and no one had ever spoken to me about them. It was the great revelation of my life. I felt immediately that it was something of exceptional importance. On the way home I hugged my treasure! I started playing them in a wonderful state of excitement, and it was only after twelve years' practice of them that I made up my mind to play them in public."[3]

Of course, Pablo was already familiar with some of the music of Bach. Like most students of the piano, he practiced Bach's *Well-Tempered Clavier*. That collection of short pieces for solo clavier (a small keyboard instrument related to the harpsichord and piano) includes selections in every major and minor key. It was therefore excellent practice for piano students, who could play it on modern instruments. Pablo was familiar with some of Bach's other music as well. But the solo cello suites had been all but forgotten over the years. Eventually, through public performances and, later, phonograph recordings, Pablo Casals made the music familiar to many people.

Throughout his five years as a student at the Municipal School of Music, Pablo continued to grow as an astonishingly talented young artist. He won many first-place prizes in the school's competitions for piano, cello, and composition. During the final year of his studies, however, he entered the darkest and most mysterious period of his life.

For reasons that are not entirely clear, at the age of fifteen Pablo became terribly depressed. He was disturbed by his parents continuing arguments over his career as a musician. But that alone could not explain the depth of his despair. He grew dissatisfied with the rites of Spain's Catholic church, although he yearned for a deeper understanding of God and religion. He anguished over the social injustices he saw all about him. He searched for answers to questions that plagued him in the church and in the writings of Socialist thinkers. But his depression only grew deeper.

"Everybody has an epoch of distress. I had it very young," he confessed. "It lasted a long time. It made me physically ill. . . . It was terrible."[4] His mental crisis reached its peak around his sixteenth birthday, near the end of 1892. He began to think of suicide, and soon could imagine little else.

It should have been a happy time for a teenager. His father had recently retired after twenty years of service as the organist of the Vendrell church. Carlos moved to Barcelona where Pablo lived, and soon found many new students willing to pay for piano lessons. Doña Pilar had just given birth to her eleventh and last child. The family lived together in an apartment in the Calle de Paleyo.

But despite his success at school, the reunion of his family, and his growing local fame, Pablo's profound sadness grew and grew. More than anyone else, Doña Pilar seemed to sense his condition. In the spring of 1893, as soon as her son graduated from music school, Pilar sent a letter to Isaac Albéniz. The time had come, she said, to use the famed musician's three-year-old letter introducing Pablo to the powerful Count de Morphy. For the sake of her son's mental health, she felt the need to act quickly.

In May, the mother brought sixteen-year-old Pablo and her two younger sons to the Barcelona train station. There, the four boarded a train bound for Madrid, the capital of Spain. The train trip took approximately twenty-four hours. But the trip directly from Madrid's Estación del Norte to the spacious suburban town house of the Count de Morphy took only an hour.

Count Guillermo de Morphy was a fascinating man, a rich and well-educated music lover who proved to be a good friend to Pablo Casals. He was actually Irish. Years earlier, he changed his name from Murphy to Morphy to make it sound more Spanish. He was also an aide and favorite of

Spain's royal family, including Queen Mother María Cristina and King Alfonso XIII, a young boy at the time.

From their very first meeting, Pablo Casals and Count de Morphy became friends. The count asked the young cellist to play almost at once, and was deeply impressed. Arrangements were made for a concert at the royal palace, where Pablo played in a string quartet. One of the selections was his own composition.

"The next morning," Pablo recalled, "the count had important and exciting news for my mother and me. The queen, he told us, had decided to give me a scholarship. It amounted to 250 pesetas—about $50.00—a month. That was not such a small amount then—in fact, it was quite a handsome sum in those days. Even so, it was not a great deal when it came to meeting the needs of a family of four. We lived very poorly."[5]

Doña Pilar and her three sons settled into a small apartment on a street opposite Madrid's royal palace. For the next two-and-a-half years, Count de Morphy personally guided Pablo's education. Every morning, the count provided instruction on subjects including literature, history, mathematics, geography, and languages. "The count contended that in order to be a fully developed artist, one had to have a full understanding of life,"[6] Pablo explained.

At the same time, Pablo attended the Madrid Conservatory of Music. He studied composition with Thomás Bretón, whose operas were popular then but are largely forgotten now. He studied chamber music with Jesús de Monasterio, an elderly violinist Pablo regarded as a superb teacher.

During school holidays, the young cellist joined other musicians to give chamber music concerts. He often traveled to towns in the Spanish countryside, where the concerts, and particularly his own playing, drew rave reviews from newspaper critics.

"Señor Casals deserves a separate paragraph," wrote one reporter, "he is a true celebrity . . . at barely eighteen years old he can proclaim himself *Maestro* and create true beauty with the violoncello . . . when he plays, one closes one's eyes and hears, more than a work of art made by human hands, music that seems the miracle of a spirit."[7] Other newspaper critics were equally struck by Casals's almost magical playing.

One of the young man's biggest fans was Queen María Cristina. She awarded the eighteen-year-old cellist the Medal of Isabel la Católica. It was a great honor for any artist. For a musician as young as Pablo, it was a stunning achievement.

Perhaps more than anyone else, Pilar Casals understood that the cello was her son's true calling. During his time in Madrid, however, Pablo did not seem to have a genuine cello teacher. After Doña Pilar and her sons had lived in the Spanish capital for nearly three years, she decided that Pablo should concentrate more on that instrument. She suggested returning to Barcelona.

Count de Morphy hated the idea. He wanted Pablo to remain in Madrid to concentrate on musical composition. He felt the young man could become a great opera composer.

Doña Pilar said, "I believe that with Pablo the cello comes before everything else. If his future is to be that of a composer, it can always come later, and his work on the cello won't interfere. But if he fails to concentrate on the instrument now, it will prove a serious disadvantage later."[8]

A great argument began, once again with young Pablo's musical future at its center. Count de Morphy found an ally in Carlos Casals. Pablo's father argued, again, that his wife's advice was unwise.

Finally, a compromise was reached. It was agreed that Pablo would travel to the city of Brussels in Belgium. There, he could study both composition and cello at the Conservatory of Music. The cello department in the Brussels school was considered Europe's best. Count de Morphy added that the Spanish queen would continue Pablo's scholarship while he studied in Brussels.

Early in autumn 1895, Pablo, his mother, and his two younger brothers traveled to Paris and then to Brussels. Pablo brought with him a glowing letter of introduction from Count de Morphy. The letter praised his abilities both as a composer and as a cellist.

To his dismay, Pablo discovered that the elderly director of the Belgian school was no longer accepting composition students. Nevertheless, the director agreed to look over some of Pablo's written compositions. He agreed they showed considerable talent. He suggested that the young cellist travel to Paris. That French city, he said, was the center of serious music. As the meeting continued, Doña Pilar pointed out that her son's scholarship required him to study at the conservatory. Finally the director arranged a meeting for the following day with Edouard Jacobs, the conservatory's advanced cello teacher.

Thinking that he was going only to an interview, and would not be expected to play an instrument, Pablo traveled alone to the conservatory the next morning. At the time, he probably thought more about his halting French, which he would have to use, than music. When he arrived, Professor Jacobs was already leading a cello class. Pablo sat in the back of the room as various students played musical selections on their cellos.

Pablo understood that he was in the midst of one of Europe's most renowned music classes. The students there all seemed to feel very important. And yet the music Pablo heard was not that impressive. There were some obvious mistakes, most uncorrected by the teacher. And the playing, in general, seemed stiff at some times and overly dramatic at others. Much of it was not entirely in tune.

As the class was coming to an end, Professor Jacobs seemed to notice Pablo for the first time. "You are the little Spaniard?" he asked. "It seems you play the cello, and the director has asked me to hear you."

Pablo was surprised that he was expected to play. But he answered quickly. "Yes," he said, "if you please."

"Have you your cello?" the teacher asked.

"No, Monsieur."

"Can you play one we have here?"

"Yes," Pablo answered, "I will try."

"What will you play?"

"Anything you like," Pablo said sincerely. He saw the curl of a cruel laugh starting on the teacher's lips.

"Well, well, you *must* be remarkable," Professor Jacobs sneered. The other students began to laugh out loud. Pablo was frozen with embarrassment. "So you can play anything *I* like!" the professor said. He decided to challenge the young Spaniard by naming many different cello pieces.

"Can you play the Servais Concerto?"

"Yes."

"Romberg? Golterman?"

To each challenge, and many others, Pablo answered yes.

"But you must be *wonderful!*" Professor Jacobs taunted him.

Greatly annoyed by the teacher's wisecracks, Pablo merely suggested that he be allowed to play. "Very well, then," the professor said, "let us hear *Souvenir de Spa*." The teacher had named a very difficult piece of music, but Pablo knew *Souvenir de Spa* very well. "Now, young gentlemen," Professor Jacobs added, "we will hear something very surprising from this young man who plays everything."[9]

Many of the students were still laughing as Pablo began playing the difficult piece on a borrowed cello. But the instant he began to play, the laughter stopped. Suddenly, the teacher and his proud students had nothing to joke about.

When Pablo finished playing, Professor Jacobs stared for several seconds and then asked him to come to his office. Pablo followed. When both men were inside the little room, the teacher closed the door and sat behind his desk. "Young man," Professor Jacobs said, "I can tell you that you have a great talent. If you study here, and if you consent to be in my class, I can promise you that you will be awarded First Prize of the conservatory. Mind you, it's not exactly according to regulations for me to tell you this at this time, but I can give you my word."

The speech did little to lessen Pablo's anger. "You were rude to me, sir," he said. "You ridiculed me in front of your pupils. I do not want to remain here one second longer."[10]

The shocked professor could do nothing but open the door as Pablo walked out of his office. For years, Professor Jacobs had to live with the shameful fact that he had once made fun of the world's finest cellist.

Pablo, with his mother and two brothers, left for Paris the next day. He had seen enough of Brussels and the famous Conservatory of Music there. But he also knew that serious difficutly lay ahead. By leaving the Brussels school, he was in danger of losing his scholarship from Queen María Cristina. It was the only source of income for himself, his mother, and his two younger brothers.

But it did not matter. At this moment and for the rest of his long life, Pablo Casals did whatever he thought was right, regardless of the consequences.

Chapter 4

STRUGGLE AND FAME

Pablo Casals and his family arrived in Paris on a sunny autumn day in 1895. After finding an inexpensive place to stay, he wrote a long letter to the Count de Morphy. He explained what had happened in Brussels, hoping that the queen would understand.

When he received the count's reply, his worst fears were realized. He must return immediately to Belgium, the count warned, or the scholarship would end. But Casals's reasons for refusing to return to the Brussels school cut deeper than his unkind reception there. Artistically, he disliked the cello playing he heard in Professor Jacobs's classroom. He felt that, as a serious artist seeking to perfect his craft, he simply could not return. Unfortunately, the scholarship from Queen María Cristina was canceled immediately.

"Those were trying days in Paris!" he remembered. "We had counted on the pension, and without it we were virtually stranded—my mother, my two young brothers and I. We had no means of support. What were we to do? My father, who now of course worried more than ever about us, could afford to send us practically nothing."[1]

The family was forced to move into a tiny apartment in a

Paris slum. Doña Pilar took in sewing, but there wasn't enough money for decent food. Pablo quickly found a job playing the cello in a Paris dance hall, but the wages were only four francs per day, hardly enough for even one person to survive. When winter arrived, the young man discovered that he could not stand cold temperatures. He promptly became very sick. Now, he was unable to work.

"One day," Casals said, "from my bed I saw my mother come in with her hair cut short. I looked at her in astonishment.

"'What's the matter?' she said. 'This is nothing.'

"For a little money, she had sold her magnificent hair. But she did not make any fuss about it, and thought it had no importance at all."[2]

Finally, the family decided to return to Barcelona. Carlos was able to scrape together enough money for train tickets, and promptly sent it. He was overjoyed that his family had finally returned, but he also was worried. Their entire life savings, modest as it was, had been wiped out.

Pablo's return to Barcelona came at a particularly difficult time for another well-known cellist. His old teacher at the city's music school, Josep García, had been caught in a scandal with a married woman. García was hastily preparing to move to Argentina.

In a matter of months, nineteen-year-old Pablo took over García's classes at the Municipal School of Music, began teaching all his private students, was hired to replace García at church services, was given another teaching position at a second music school, and was appointed principal cellist in an opera orchestra.

One man's misfortune had brought Pablo some much-needed good luck! Suddenly he had more work than he could handle. For the first time, there was plenty of money to share with his family. With part of his rapidly growing earnings, he helped Carlos, Pilar, and his younger brothers move into a nicer house along the Plaza de Cataluña in Barcelona.

His improved finances came at a good time. According to Spanish law, he was at an age when he was required to join the army. The Casals family, especially Doña Pilar, had little respect for the military. (She later told one of her younger sons that he was not born to kill or be killed. She insisted that he flee the country rather than enter the army and fight in a war.) Fortunately, Pablo faced an easier decision. In Spain at that time, it was legal to pay money to government authorities to avoid military service. Pablo Casals did so without hesitation.

The following summer, he was invited to play at a casino in Portugal. He accepted, in part, because he realized that he would have to travel near Madrid. He could visit Count de Morphy.

"The moment I arrived in Madrid, I hurried to his house,"

Pablo said. "He welcomed me as a son. We talked and talked—it was as if there had never been any difficulty between us."[3]

During the same trip through Madrid, he had a happy reunion with Queen María Cristina as well. He told the queen about his problems in Brussels and about his even more serious problems in Paris. María Cristina was deeply moved. She asked him to play at the palace. After the recital, the queen talked to him once again.

"Pablo," she said, "I want to give you something that you can always keep as a remembrance of me. I want it to be something you can touch." She placed a finger next to her beautiful bracelet. "Which of these stones do you like best?"

Casals answered, "They are all so beautiful, Your Majesty."

Pointing to a large and beautiful sapphire the queen said, "Then you shall have this one."[4]

The cellist never forgot the kindness of the queen. Some time later, he had the valuable gem mounted on his cello bow.

The concert at the casino was a tremendous success. Casals became so well known throughout the nation that Portugal's King Carlos and Queen Marie-Amélie asked him to play for them. Casals was so excited by another royal performance that he forgot to bring his cello to the palace. The king and queen smiled at his forgetfulness, sending a servant for the cello. On his return to Spain, Queen María Cristina presented him with a valuable old cello made by a master craftsman named Gagliano. She also gave him his second royal medal, the Order of Carlos III. He was twenty years old.

During the same visit to Madrid, in November 1897, Casals for the first time played solo cello accompanied by a full symphony orchestra. He played the Cello Concerto in D minor by the French composer Edouard Lalo. The Madrid Symphony was conducted by Thomás Bretón, Pablo's old composition teacher at the city's Conservatory of Music.

Remarkably, the concert received only polite applause. Audiences of the day were accustomed to well-known musicians who behaved like showmen. Great virtuosos of the violin and other instruments often wore long, flowing hair, flashy capes, and brilliant jewelry. Some resorted to tricks such as playing their instruments upside down. One notable soloist even pretended to let his priceless violin fall to the floor while the orchestra played, catching it at the last instant.

Pablo Casals was a great musician, but he had no interest in audience-pleasing games. Even as a young man, he was already beginning to lose his hair. There would be no flowing locks of hair bobbing furiously to the music at his concerts. In fact there would be few distractions of any sort to compete with the music he played so beautifully.

When he returned to Barcelona, Casals formed a string

quartet with three other musicians. Included in the group were the Belgian violinist Mathieu Crickboom and two other Spaniards, violist Rafael Gálvez and the well-known pianist and composer Enrique Granados. The group performed chamber music concerts to wildly approving audiences in Barcelona, Madrid, Valencia, and other cities. In one review, a Barcelona newspaper devoted most of its space to praising Casals. "Short of stature, like that of a boy," the report noted, "he is transformed into a giant when he plays."[5]

As Pablo's fame continued to grow, the government of Spain and its armed forces became the source of worldwide controversy. For several years, Spanish soldiers had been fighting in Cuba to keep control of that large island. In December 1897, the United States battleship *Maine* was sent to Cuba to defend American lives and interests there. On the night of February 15, 1898, a huge explosion aboard the ship caused it to sink in Havana harbor. A total of 266 lives were lost. The cause of the explosion was never discovered, but many Americans blamed it on Spanish troops.

A little more than two months later, the United States Congress declared war on Spain, with the intent of freeing Cuba from Spanish control. In a matter of months, Spanish fleets from Puerto Rico to the Philippine Islands had been soundly beaten by American forces. A peace treaty was signed in Paris on December 10, 1898. As part of the agreement, Spain gave up control of Cuba and gave to the United

States Puerto Rico, Guam, and the large group of Pacific islands called the Philippines.

"Like the rest of the people of Spain," Casals remembered, "we Catalans of course knew about the military campaigns that had been dragging on in Cuba for several years to suppress the rebellion against Spanish rule—there were, after all, almost a quarter of a million Spanish troops in Cuba at the time. But few Spaniards realized what losses their army was suffering, from the guerrilla warfare in the swamps and jungles and especially from malaria, yellow fever and other tropical diseases. These facts were kept from the people, and while the casualties grew, the newspapers reported sweeping successes."[6]

When the United States entered the war, Spanish forces in both the Atlantic and the Pacific quickly crumbled. "I was in Barcelona at the time," Casals recalled. "Shortly after news of the defeat, transport ships arrived in the port carrying remnants of the Spanish army. For days, thousands of soldiers—the sick, the maimed, and those ravaged by hunger and disease—wandered through the streets of the city. The horror of it! . . . And for what, I asked myself, for what?"[7]

During Casals's long lifetime, his beloved Catalonia, all of Spain, and much of the world suffered through more brutal wars. But around the time of the Spanish-American conflict, Pablo met a group of people who helped him through the most troubling of times.

In the mountains near Barcelona is a famous monastery called *Montserrat*, which means "serrated mountain." The monastery was built near the top of the rocky mountain more than a thousand years ago, in the ninth century. Pablo had long talks with the religious men who lived on the craggy mountain. He regarded many of them as his friends. In his talks with the monks of Montserrat, he tried to understand the world about him.

Throughout his life, Casals wrote a great deal of music. He only allowed a small fraction of it to be published during his lifetime. What was published was prepared and printed by the monks of Montserrat.

By 1899, Pablo had earned enough money in Barcelona to set up his family in comfortable conditions. He decided it was time to travel again. Carrying a letter of introduction from the Count de Morphy, he went to Paris. There, he stayed briefly in the home of a famous American singer whose stage name was Emma Nevada. When Pablo arrived, Emma was planning to leave for London, where she was scheduled to sing in a number of concerts. At her urging, Casals agreed to travel with her.

In London, Pablo played a concerto by the French composer Camille Saint-Saëns. The concert was held in a famous glass building known as the Crystal Palace. There, an aide for England's Queen Victoria heard him and asked him to play for the queen. The young cellist quickly agreed.

The concert took place on the Isle of Wight, an island just off the southern coast of England. At Osborne House, the summer home of Queen Victoria, Pablo played for an audience that included the queen; the Prince of Wales, who soon became King Edward VII; and the Duke of York, who eventually became King George V.

After he returned to Paris, Casals went to see Charles Lamoureux, the aged but famous conductor of the Lamoureux Orchestra. The old conductor was a brilliant, busy, and sometimes temperamental character. When Pablo was led into his Paris study, he pretended not to notice him. Lamoureux was studying the score for his premiere of the opera *Tristan and Isolde* by Richard Wagner. Unsure what to do, Casals finally said, "Sir, I don't wish to disturb you. I only came to give you this letter from the Count de Morphy."

The frail conductor moved his body with difficulty. He held out his hand and Casals gave him the letter. Lamoureux read it and then said, "All right, you come tomorrow with a pianist and your 'cello."

When Casals arrived at his office the next day, however, the famous conductor seemed once again not to notice him.

"As I don't wish to disturb you," Pablo said, "I shall go immediately."

"Young man," Lamoureux said, "I am interested in you. Play me the Lalo concerto." Pablo had recently played the piece in Madrid and knew it well. As soon as he began to play, the conductor dropped his papers and stared at him. When he had finished, Lamoureux said, "My dear child, you are one of the elect."[8] Lamoureux made arrangements for a concert to be held with Pablo Casals as soloist. It was a smashing success. Another concert was scheduled and performed.

With these appearances, Pablo Casals became famous. "Almost overnight," he remembered, "following my concerts with Lamoureux, wide recognition came to me. I was besieged with requests to play at concerts and recitals. Suddenly all doors were open to me."[9]

As the nineteenth century ended, Pablo was at the start of a long era of fame. But there was sadness too. Before his first concert with Lamoureux came news that the Count de Morphy had died in almost total poverty. On December 21, 1899, Charles Lamoureux also died. Despite his many triumphs, Casals never forgot those who had helped him along the way to fame.

Chapter 5

MUSIC AROUND THE WORLD

At the turn of the century, Paris was the artistic and musical center of the Western world. His international fame secured by his concerts with the Lamoureux Orchestra, Casals became friendly with many different artists, musicians, and writers living there. During the same period, he traveled a great deal, giving concerts in London and in various countries on the European mainland.

Casals agreed to leave Paris in 1901 for an eighty-concert tour of the United States with the famous singer Emma Nevada. He boarded the steamship *St. Paul* and crossed the Atlantic, arriving in New York harbor on November 16, 1901. With him were Emma Nevada and her husband and two other European musicians. Also accompanying the group was Raymond Duncan, who worked as Emma's secretary and as a kind of manager for the concerts. Duncan was the brother of the famous American dancer Isadora Duncan.

It was Pablo Casals's first trip to America. "The New World ceased to be a phrase to me," he said. "Newness abounded on all sides. One sensed a nation still in the process of coming into being, like a great symphony in rehearsal."[1]

In large and even some smaller cities all across America,

Casals and the other musicians gave their concerts. Emma Nevada was the headliner. She sang selections from operas, but also sang popular tunes of the day, including "Home, Sweet Home" and "Listen to the Mockingbird." Casals and several other musicians also played instrumental solos.

The musical company traveled through Rhode Island and upstate New York and then moved southward. During all the travels, Casals wanted to do more than give concerts and rest in his hotel room. He was anxious to see the sights in America. With Léon Moreau, the young pianist who accompanied Emma Nevada, he shared a number of adventures.

In Baltimore, Casals watched a professional boxing match, but found it too rough for his taste. In Wilkes-Barre, Pennsylvania, Casals and Moreau toured a coal mine. Forgetting the time, they arrived at the concert hall too late to wash. Some members of the audience noted a surprising amount of coal dust on stage that evening.

The traveling musicians reached Texas in January 1902. "The Wild West was still a reality in those days—" Casals recalled, "when I now watch cowboy programs on television, I'm reminded of some of the Western towns where we gave concerts on that tour. Great excitement would attend our arrival. There would be large streamers over the streets announcing the concert, and printed posters on the walls of buildings—sometimes next to a poster offering a reward for some wanted outlaw."[2]

In a small Texas ranching town, Casals and Moreau decided to spend the afternoon looking around. Although Pablo seldom drank alcohol, he decided to enter a saloon there. Before long, the two Europeans were involved in a game of dice. The other players wore guns and huge ammo belts. To his great surprise, Casals began to win quite a bit of money.

For a time, the Texas cowboys seemed to enjoy the company of the European strangers. A number of free drinks were offered, but Casals politely declined. But as the stacks of silver dollars in front of him grew larger, some of the cowboys grew uneasy. When Pablo refused yet another free drink, a man said, "Here we bet *and* drink."[3]

Fortunately, just as the Texans were becoming rowdy, the dice seemed to turn against Casals. As he began losing money, the tension eased. The game ended in good humor.

From Texas, the musicians boarded a train to the Territory of New Mexico, where Casals persuaded Moreau to explore the desert on foot. The cellist was enchanted by the desert, and wanted to walk on and on. But Moreau was anxious to return to the hotel. As they were about to turn around, Casals spotted a lonely cabin in the distance. Hot and tired, the two men arrived at the cabin about a half hour later. They were greeted by a man and a woman. Although the settler was dressed like a cowboy, Pablo noted that he had an unusual accent.

"You are not of this country," Casals said to him.

"No," the man answered, "I come from across the water."

"And from where?"

"Oh," the man said to his visitors, "it's a country you never heard of."

"And what is the name of the country?" Casals persisted.

"Its name," the man answered, "is Catalonia."[4] For a time, the two Catalans who had met in the American wilderness talked about the old country. But the visit was all too brief, because the whirlwind tour had to continue.

In Arizona Territory, Casals was so enchanted by the Grand Canyon that he rode a mule down the steep cliffs to the Colorado River. Soon, the musicians traveled on to California, where a concert was given on February 11, 1902. Then they traveled up the Pacific coast to San Francisco.

Even in 1902, San Francisco was a sophisticated city, remarkably so for the American West. Just a few decades earlier, it had been a part of the American frontier. From his first sight of the city, Casals fell in love with San Francisco.

His visit to the beautiful city almost ended his career. One afternoon, he and some friends decided to climb a mountain across San Francisco Bay. As they were on the way down the hill, a boulder suddenly came loose and headed straight for Casals. Warned by another climber, he was able to get most of his body out of the way. Unfortunately, the boulder fell on his left hand, smashing it instantly. As he looked at his wounded hand, Pablo had a most peculiar reaction. "Thank God," he thought, "I shall not play the 'cello anymore."[5]

It may seem like an unusual reaction for a young man already enjoying worldwide fame as a cellist. "You see," Casals explained much later, "if one decides to play an instrument conscientiously with all seriousness, one becomes a slave for life. . . . I thought I would give up my life to composition and conducting."[6] Although he loved music, his relationship with the cello was a difficult and demanding one. Before all of his concerts throughout his life, Pablo Casals suffered from stage fright. The fear only passed after he began to play.

After the accident, it seemed as if he would no longer have to worry about concert jitters. Doctors who examined him said that he would never regain full use of his injured hand. Emma Nevada and the other musicians were forced to continue the tour without him.

His hand covered with a plaster cast, Casals recuperated as a guest of Michael Stein, president of the Bay City cable car company. As the months went by, he also formed a friendship with his host's younger sister, Gertrude. At the time, Gertrude was studying medicine. A few years later, however, she attained worldwide fame as a writer. At around the same time, he formed an even more lasting friendship with a pianist named Theresa Hermann. She had been one of his companions on the unfortunate mountain-climbing expedition.

Despite the sad predictions by doctors, Casals began exercising his injured hand as soon as the cast was removed. After only four months, he gained sufficient strength to practice the cello once again. Although the scar on his fingering hand remained for the rest of his life, little permanent damage was done. He was able to resume his career.

By the time Pablo Casals returned to Europe in June 1902, his hand had healed completely. He lived in Paris but often visited Spain. In fact he spent the next four decades constantly traveling, giving concerts all over the world. Traveling by train and steamship, he visited an endless list of cities: London, Venice, Stockholm, New York, Washington, Philadelphia, São Paulo, Buenos Aires, St. Petersburg, Madrid, and on and on.

"I lost track of the number of concerts I gave," he remembered. "I do know it was often around two hundred and fifty a year. Sometimes when I was traveling in countries where cities were close together I'd give over thirty concerts a month—on Sundays I would often have one concert in the afternoon and another in the evening. It was a demanding schedule. I never missed an engagement. I had a strong constitution, but even so I sometimes felt exhausted. Once, in Berlin, I fainted in the middle of a performance, but after a short rest I finished the concert."[7]

He gave many of his concerts with a talented pianist named Harold Bauer. Bauer began studying music as a violinist, but soon switched to the piano. Casals and Bauer traveled over much of the world, although the latter suffered terribly from seasickness.

During a second tour of the United States in 1904, Casals played for President Theodore Roosevelt. Soon after his return to Europe, he formed a musical partnership with two other superb musicians. One was a Swiss pianist named Alfred Cortot, the second the French violinist Jacques Thibaud. For at least one month a year during the next three decades, Casals, Cortot, and Thibaud gave celebrated concerts of chamber music all over the world.

The trio also did much to popularize an astounding new invention: the phonograph machine. Thomas Edison had first developed tinfoil phonograph recordings just a few months after Casals was born. But improvements in the device around the turn of the century made it possible, for the first time, to enjoy recorded music. Pablo made his first phonograph recording around 1903. During the next six decades he made hundreds more.

Early recordings were made under difficult circumstances. Musicians had to huddle around a large horn. At the bottom of the horn, the narrowest part, was a needle that scratched the surface of a rotating disk. A similar machine was used to listen to the finished recording. The sound was scratchy and tinny, but it was nevertheless regarded as a miracle.

During Casals's long career, recorded sound was improved dramatically. By the 1950s, electronic microphones, amplifiers, and tape recorders made recordings far easier to produce and more realistic to hear. By the 1960s, stereophonic sound and high-fidelity equipment made recordings sound nearly as good as the original performance. Nevertheless, Casals always regarded recordings as a compromise. He preferred live performances of music throughout his life.

A number of Pablo's most notable live performances were made in Russia in the early 1900s. His first series of Russian concerts was held in 1905, at a time when many people were rebelling against the rule of Russian czars. For more than a decade, political problems and, soon enough, open warfare rocked the nation. Pablo himself noted the heavy-handed techniques of the czar's secret police, who seemed to be everywhere. Nevertheless, he visited Russia often. He worked with a number of famous Russian composers, including Sergei Rachmaninoff, Nikolai Rimsky-Korsakov, and Alexander Scriabin.

At a concert in Brussels, Casals created an incident that caused a great deal of excitement among professional musicians. At the Brussels Conservatory of Music, and many other places in Europe, the public was often invited to buy tickets to final orchestra rehearsals. Although audiences were generally large, the musicians themselves were only paid for the actual concert, not the dress rehearsal. Pablo decided that this was unfair.

During a final rehearsal in Brussels, Pablo continually stopped playing. The orchestra accompanying him soon stopped as well. He asked many questions of the conductor, pointing out the need for a number of changes. The audience grew restless, expecting to hear music with few, if any, interruptions.

For the second half of the rehearsal/concert, Casals was scheduled to play one of Bach's suites for solo cello. However, Casals had been practicing this music of Bach ever since he and his father had discovered it when he was a youth. He had no need to practice it again, and he refused to do so. "I have already practiced my Bach Suite," he told the director, "and do not need to rehearse it now." Confronted by an even longer delay, the audience became more impatient than ever. Soon enough, there were shouts from the auditorium seats.

The director became frantic. "Mr. Casals, I am obliged to *beg* you to play your Bach; the audience is expecting it. This means another concert fee and you may consider yourself engaged for the two." With this new agreement, Casals played the remainder of the program.

Remarkably, he refused to keep the extra wages he had won. "This, the fee agreed upon, I will keep," he told the director, "but here is the second one you gave me; it must go to the orchestra."[8] He had won an important point. From that time on, musicians in Brussels, and many other cities as well, would be paid for all performances attended by a paying audience.

Most professional musicians heartily agreed with the stand Casals took in Brussels. But an incident in Paris in 1912 was more controversial. There, Casals was scheduled to play a concerto by the Czech composer Antonin Dvorák. The Concerts Colonne orchestra was conducted by Gabriel Pierné.

Just before the dress rehearsal, Casals and Pierné were talking in Pablo's dressing room. "What a ghastly piece of music!" Pierné said about the Dvorák concerto. "It's hardly worth playing. It's not really music at all."

Casals was shocked. "Are you out of your mind?" the cellist asked. "How can you talk that way about such a magnificent work?"

As the discussion grew more heated, Pierné added: "You're enough of a musician to know how bad the music is." Casals could barely contain his anger.

"If that's the way you feel about the work," he said, "then you're clearly not capable of conducting it. Since I happen to love the music, I couldn't take part in its desecration. And I won't. I refuse to play."

The two men continued arguing. As the audience grew

more restless, Pablo spotted the famous French composer Claude Debussy standing near the stage. "Ask Debussy if he thinks any artist could perform under the circumstances," Casals said to Pierné. The director posed the question to his fellow Frenchman. Casals was even more shocked by Debussy's answer.

"If you really wanted to play, you could," Debussy said.

"That may be your opinion, Monsieur Debussy," Casals replied, "but I can tell you I haven't the slightest intention of doing so."[9]

Casals gathered his things and quickly stormed out of the hall. The next day, he received legal papers indicating that he was being sued for breach of contract. When the case eventually came to court, he was fined three thousand francs.

It had been expensive, but once again Pablo Casals felt it was necessary to stand up for a principle. It would not be the last time he was forced to pay a heavy price for his beliefs.

Pablo Casals with his cello
in 1915.

In 1914 Casals married
Susan Scott Metcalfe, an
American singer.

On his eightieth birthday, Casals joked with some of the residents of Prades, in France, just across the border from Spain.

In 1959 Casals plays a game of bowling

Practice was an important part of Casals's life.

Casals talks with music students from North and South America at his home in San Juan, Puerto Rico.

Above: Pablo Casals and Alexander Schneider talk about the 1959 Festival Casals, held in Puerto Rico.
Below: Casals was respected for his conducting and for his cello virtuosity.

It was a solemn occasion in 1961 when the White House paid tribute to Pablo Casals (above). But when Casals played "Mary Had a Little Lamb" with comedian Jack Benny (below), Casals had to hold back his laughter.

Casals and Rudolf Serkin, artistic director of the Marlboro Music School and Festival in Vermont, chat.

Rehearsing with the London Philharmonic Orchestra at Royal Festival Hall, London, in 1963

Casals and his wife, Marta, arrive in
New York in 1970.

In Puerto Rico, Casals strolls along
the beach with an umbrella to
protect him from the sun.

At the age of 95, Casals plays the piano in the early morning, as he did each day.

Pablo Casals conducts the Orchestra of the Festival Casals while Isaac Stern and Rudolf Serkin play violins.

In 1971 Pablo Casals was given the United Nations Peace Medal from United Nations Secretary-General U Thant. Casals composed a piece called "Hymn to the United Nations" to commemorate the twenty-sixth anniversary of the United Nations.

Chapter 6

WAR AND PAU

Some newspaper critics called Casals a temperamental genius. Pablo insisted he was neither moody nor touchy. He was clearly, however, a musical genius. By the second decade of the twentieth century, Pablo Casals was an international celebrity. He was also rich. By 1910, construction was already underway for a home, later vastly enlarged, that became known as *Villa Casals* "the House of Casals." It was built under the supervision of Doña Casals on the beach at San Salvador, where Pablo had spent so much time as a child. Unfortunately, his father never lived to see the lovely home built. Carlos died in 1906. Although Pablo lived and traveled all over the world, he had many happy vacations with his aging mother at the beautiful home.

During a concert in Berlin in 1913, according to Casals, he met an American singer named Susan Scott Metcalfe. (A number of reporters noted that the pair may have met earlier. Both had appeared at the same concert in New York in 1904.) At any rate, the cellist and the American singer developed a strong friendship immediately after the Berlin concert. They were married in Susan's hometown of New Rochelle, New York, on March 4, 1914.

Pablo's dear friend Enrique Granados, the well-known composer with whom he often played chamber music, sent congratulations. "I cannot tell you how joyously my life moves . . . ," Casals answered him, "all is changed for me and already I can see it in my face."[1] Soon after their marriage, Pablo and Susan gave a number of joint concerts in the United States and Europe.

"We were, however, ill-suited to one another," he admitted, "and our relationship was short-lived, though it was some years before we were divorced. Our life together was not a happy one. But these, of course, are things one does not discuss."[2]

During the fateful year of 1914, the problems between Pablo and his wife paled in comparison to a world that seemed to be unraveling. During the summer of that year, World War I began in Europe, gradually spreading over much of the globe.

"I was in Paris when the war broke out," Casals said. "The city went berserk. One would have thought there might be some awareness of the terrible calamity that had overtaken the country, but no, on the contrary, there was a wildly festive mood. Bands playing martial music, flags flying from every window, bombastic speeches about glory and patriotism! . . . Who knows how many of those young men who paraded smiling through the streets of Paris died in muddy trenches, or came home crippled for life? And in how many other cities and countries were similar parades taking place?"[3]

For Pablo Casals and his musical associates, casualties of war came quickly. The famed violinist Fritz Kreisler was drafted into the Austrian army and wounded on the Russian Front. In 1916, Enrique Granados and wife were killed when their ship was torpedoed in the English Channel. The pianist Harold Bauer fled to the United States.

To escape the savage fighting in Europe, Pablo spent much of his time during the war years living in New York City. At the Metropolitan Opera House there, Casals took part in a concert to raise money for the Granados's six children. On May 7, 1916, with violinist Fritz Kreisler and the legendary pianist Ignace Jan Paderewski, he played the Beethoven Trio in B Flat. Thousands of people, unable to purchase tickets for the sold-out performance, lined the sidewalks outside the opera house. During the war years, Pablo gave many other concerts, especially in American cities.

World War I ended in 1918. Approximately thirty million people had died or had been wounded for the cause of international patriotism.

The following year, 42-year-old Pablo Casals returned to Paris, the city he had left in haste shortly after the outbreak of war. At the time he left, he had placed all his personal belongings, including books, musical scores, and letters, in a warehouse for safekeeping. He soon discovered that French police had opened all his boxes, scattering the contents over the floor. Gone were personal letters he had cherished from many musicians and composers, including Enrique Granados, Camille Saint-Saëns, Richard Strauss, and many others. He never learned what the police had been looking for.

The tragedies of war were many, and Casals was lucky to have only lost a few friends and his personal papers. Now, he was about to begin one of the happiest periods of his life.

In the autumn of 1919, he returned to Spain and his beloved Catalonia. He planned to make Barcelona and San Salvador his home for the rest of his life. That life, of course, would be spent involved almost entirely in music.

Although he was best known as a cellist, Casals already was an experienced conductor of symphony orchestras. He had, for example, directed rehearsals of a Granados opera while he was still a teenager. He became interested in mastering what he called the greatest instrument of them all: a full orchestra.

At the time he returned to Catalonia, the city of Barcelona had two orchestras. Unfortunately, neither group scheduled regular performances. Rehearsals for either were rare. The quality of the music necessarily suffered. "I talked to the conductors," Casals said, "telling them I would finance them and play with them in order to form a really first-class ensemble, but they kept on saying that it could not be done and that I had been away too long from Catalonia to know the real conditions there."[4] Casals was shocked to learn that the conductors had little interest in improving their own orchestras!

Finally Pablo decided to organize his own orchestra. But he found nothing but trouble wherever he turned. "Wherever I sought cooperation—among professors at the music schools, composers, civic leaders—I was told another orchestra wasn't wanted or it wasn't feasible. The press carried articles ridiculing my idea. Practically no one was willing to offer financial backing. One wealthy man told me, "I prefer bullfighting to music anyway."[5]

It was clear that, outside of a few close friends and his immediate family, Pablo would find little help forming a new orchestra. He finally decided to do it on his own. He began searching throughout Barcelona and nearby villages for talented musicians. He held hundreds of auditions, judging each only by the player's ability.

"With my own money I engaged eighty-eight musicians," he recalled, "the best I could find. They had previously been badly paid and came to rehearsals as they pleased. I promised them a good salary but told them they would have to rehearse every morning and afternoon punctually."[6]

It took several months for Pablo to find and locate the musicians for the new orchestra. When the job was completed, he decided to call the group the *Orquestra Pau Casals*. Pau, you may recall, is a Catalan word for peace and was Pablo's name in Catalan. It was natural for the cellist to use his Catalan name at this time. Soon after World War I, many Catalans hoped that Catalonia could become a true nation, not just a part of Spain. There was considerable political unrest in and around Barcelona.

Organizing the Orquestra Pau Casals had been difficult, but the greatest problem was to come. Shortly before the first rehearsals were scheduled, Pablo became extremely tired from the long months of work. He also suffered from an eye infection. Neither condition was serious, but the treatment nearly killed him. A doctor gave him an injection that made it difficult to move the muscles in his neck. A few hours later, a nurse mistakenly gave him the same injection a second time. Now, he lay in bed almost completely paralyzed. It would be impossible for him to conduct rehearsals for the new orchestra.

While he recuperated in bed, Pablo sent a message for the musicians to keep meeting at the rehearsal hall. He insisted on paying each musician's salary in full, even though he was unable to direct them. Finally, several members of the orchestra called on him.

"Maestro, what *shall* we do?" a spokesman asked.

Casals answered, "You must go to your rehearsal hall at the same time day after day and play, play, play."[7]

After resting for two months, Pablo was strong enough to leave his bed and speak to the orchestra as a whole. He thanked the musicians for standing by him during the difficult time. Noting that summer was approaching, and with it a break in the concert season, he declared that rehearsals would begin in earnest in the fall.

After a week of concentrated rehearsals that autumn, the orchestra was ready for its first concert. The premiere of the Orquestra Pau Casals was held in Barcelona's Palace of Music on October 13, 1920. The orchestra played Bach's Suite for Orchestra in D, Beethoven's Seventh Symphony, Ravel's *Mother Goose Suite*, and a tone poem by Franz Liszt. Some members of Barcelona society decided not to attend the concert, and they asked their friends and associates to do the same. There were a number of empty seats in the Palace of Music on opening night.

"Success did not come overnight," Casals said about the orchestra he formed. "We had a long struggle. . . . We gave two series of concerts a year—one in the spring, one in the autumn. In the winters I continued my own concert tours, giving performances on the cello and occasionally appearing as a guest conductor. Those tours now served a special purpose—they helped provide for my orchestra. Despite growing support from the community, seven years elapsed before the orchestra was fully self-sustaining. In the meantime, I made up each season's deficit."[8]

It is fortunate that Casals's worldwide tours earned him a fortune. In the seven or eight years it took his orchestra to earn a profit, he spent between three and four million pesetas of his own money sustaining it. It was the equivalent of millions of dollars in modern United States currency.

Pablo Casals worked with great seriousness to make the Orquestra Pau Casals an organization all Catalans could take pride in. Many of its musicians had much to learn. "Casals had to teach," said one of the orchestra members, "and he is a great teacher. He does not talk at length about style . . . he sings, he inspires. . . . At times he would ask, let us say, the first viola (an excellent musician) 'Please give me your viola,' and he would play and say 'Play it this way.'"[9]

Casals was the permanent conductor of his orchestra for seventeen years. He was forty-three years old when he began, sixty-one when, tragically, he conducted it for the last time. But he was not the orchestra's only conductor during that magnificent era. Many of the world's leading composers and conductors traveled to Barcelona to lead performances by the Orquestra Pau Casals. Among the nearly sixty guest conductors were Ernest Ansermet, Vincent d'Indy, Manuel de Falla, Otto Klemperer, Serge Koussevitzky, Pierre Monteux, Hermann Scherchen, Arnold Schönberg, Richard Strauss, and Igor Stravinsky.

Catalans were slow to accept the new orchestra. But before long, they learned that the only way to hear Pablo

Casals play the cello was to attend Orquestra Pau Casals concerts when he was a soloist. Between 1920 and 1929, Casals played nowhere else in Barcelona, with one exception. In 1926, he announced that he would give a solo cello concert for orchestra season ticket holders only. Immediately, the number of season tickets that were sold more than doubled.

In 1927, Casals held a concert to help an old friend, the Belgian violin virtuoso Eugène Ysaÿe. Ysaÿe had once been one of the world's greatest musicians, but was now seventy years old and nearly broke. Although the old man had stopped playing the violin, Casals urged him to play once more. His version of Beethoven's violin concerto, while not perfectly played, was well received by an audience that remembered his great performances of the past. After the concert, the old Belgian cried with happiness and kissed Pablo's hand.

By 1928 Casals's orchestra was finally on solid financial ground. Newspaper critics who had once made fun of the orchestra now were beginning to call it Catalonia's greatest treasure. No longer faced with a struggle for economic survival, Pablo decided to find a new audience for his concerts.

"Our music, I felt, reached too limited an audience," he said, "—largely those who were comfortably off, well-to-do. The working people, generally speaking, could not afford the concert tickets. Those few who could scrape together the money sat in the cheapest gallery seats. . . . The idea of giving free concerts didn't appeal to me. I was conscious of the dignity of working people, and I knew they had little desire to receive what might seem charity. I wanted the men and women from the factories and the shops and the waterfront to be able to hear our music and enjoy it. After all, they were the people who had produced most of the wealth of our country—why, then, should they be kept from sharing its cultural riches?"[10]

It took some time to work out all the details. Eventually, however, it was agreed that working people with limited incomes could attend a whole series of concerts for less money than the cost of a single standard ticket. By joining the Workingman's Concert Organization, men and women could enjoy the same fine music once reserved for the wealthy.

There is some confusion as to when the first workers' concert was given. Casals himself said it was in the fall of 1928. But his most significant English-language biographer, H.L. Kirk, notes that it was in May 1926. Whenever they first occurred, the concerts were an immediate and smashing success. In the beginning, twenty-five hundred people joined the Workingman's Concert Organization. By the mid-1930s its ranks had swelled to three hundred thousand Catalans! Members formed their own amateur orchestra and a large chorus as well.

Casals's work bringing great music to the masses made him a national hero. Dozens of streets and public squares throughout Catalan cities and towns were named in his honor. Although he was no longer a young man, Pablo couldn't help but enjoy his dual roles as a musical genius and a Catalan hero.

Whenever his busy schedule permitted, he took time off to relax at the San Salvador home where Doña Pilar and a younger brother and his family lived. In the late 1920s, he remodeled the home, adding many large new rooms and outbuildings. It became an impressive mansion, with beautiful artworks inside and out and impressive formal gardens.

In the winter of 1931, while Pablo was giving a series of concerts in Switzerland, his mother died. Like his father, Doña Pilar had helped Pablo immeasurably during his early years as a music student. But the sadness he felt at her death was eased by an astounding new development for Catalonia and all of Spain. Unfortunately, the new development was far too brief.

Casals listens to the news broadcast on the radio.

Chapter 7

SHATTERED DREAMS

From the earliest stages of his career, Pablo Casals had good relations with the monarchs of Spain. Queen María Cristina and, later, King Alfonso XIII, both enjoyed his artistry. It was clear, however, that Casals was not in favor of the rule of monarchs. Especially under King Alfonso, conditions in Spain deteriorated drastically. Throughout much of the 1920s, the king allowed a military dictator, General Miguel Primo de Rivera, to control the day-to-day activities of the nation. Poverty and dissatisfaction were widespread.

In the spring of 1931, the same year that Doña Pilar died, King Alfonso was forced to flee from Spain. Before the end of the year Spain had a new constitution, which guaranteed the right of all Spaniards to elect their own government. The region of Catalonia also won the right to establish its own government and to direct many of its own affairs independent of the rest of Spain. For many Catalans, including Pablo Casals, it was a dream come true.

On April 15, 1931, the day after King Alfonso left the throne of Spain, Casals conducted a joyful concert in front of seven thousand people in Barcelona. In the audience was the new president of the Catalan government, Francesc Maciá. The Orquestra Pau Casals and a large chorus performed Beethoven's Ninth Symphony. The final movement of that work includes a famous German poem, Johann Schiller's *Ode to Joy*, which was put to music by Beethoven. At the end of the concert, President Maciá arose to announce that the new republic had arrived on the wings of Schiller's joyful poem.

Pablo Casals was fifty-three years old, but for the first time in his life, he became interested in politics. He voted in national and local elections, something he had never done before. He noted with satisfaction that men of great learning, including scientists, scholars, and university professors, were elected to political offices in the new government.

The members of Spain's Republican government knew that vast education programs were needed to conquer illiteracy in the nation. In just a few years, thousands of new schools were built. The new government made it legal, for the first time since anyone could remember, to teach the Catalan language in the schools of Catalonia.

Casals was so excited by events in Spain that he cut back drastically on his worldwide tours. Of course he continued to conduct his orchestra in concerts in Barcelona and neighboring towns and cities. One trip he felt he had to take brought him to Scotland in the fall of 1934. There he met the famous missionary and musical scholar Albert Schweitzer.

Schweitzer loved the music of Bach. He played it on the organ and studied it energetically. As soon as he heard Casals play some Bach selections, Schweitzer was overwhelmed. Although almost always apart, the two men became lifelong friends. From the far corners of the world, they exchanged letters for many years.

The 1930s were years of economic depression throughout much of the world. As in many other nations, poverty, unemployment, and labor disputes were widespread throughout Spain. A number of Spanish military men, including General Francisco Franco, had been against the Republican form of government from the beginning. Charging that some members of the young administration were Communists, Franco and other generals tried to undermine Spanish democracy. They eventually hired foreign troops who brutally destroyed labor strikes, killing many workers.

General Franco believed that governments should have dictatorial powers. Military and political leaders of a number of other nations held similar views. They, like Franco, were called *Fascists.*

Life in Spain and Catalonia was becoming increasingly chaotic. Nevertheless elections held in 1936 proved that Spaniards strongly supported the Republican democracy. Members of the Republican government forced General Franco into virtual exile by giving him a post in the faraway

Canary Islands. During this tense period, Casals continued directing his orchestra and made some international tours during the off-season. But by the summer of 1936, the strained situation in Spain erupted into open warfare.

On July 18, 1936, Casals was getting ready for a final rehearsal of his orchestra in Barcelona. In a sad coincidence, the musicians were preparing to play, once again, Beethoven's Ninth Symphony. The performance would be given in the same hall used for the concert Pablo conducted on the day the Spanish republic was born just over five years earlier.

"The final rehearsal took place at the Orfeó Català on the evening of July 18," he remembered. "I shall never, never forget that day. In the morning word came over the radio from Madrid that there had been a military uprising in Morocco—an uprising staged by fascist generals who were reported to be planning a nationwide insurrection in Spain and the overthrow of the Republican government. All day tension had mounted in Barcelona and rumors ran wild. . . . Nobody knew what the situation really was. By nightfall the avenues and plazas were thronged with people—with soldiers, Civil Guards, factory workers in overalls, and crowds of agitated men and women. Everybody's radio was on. Over loudspeakers set up in the streets, messages were being broadcast by the government: *'Do not turn your radios off! Stay calm! Traitors are spreading wild rumors to sow fear and panic! Keep tuned in! The Republic is in control of the situation!"* [1]

As he hurried through the crowded streets to the rehearsal hall, Casals worried that the Republican government would not be able to control the situation. In tense circumstances, he led the orchestra through the first three movements of Beethoven's great symphony. But as the large chorus was gathering for the final movement, he was handed a message from a government official.

The message noted that a battle was expected to begin at any time in Barcelona. The rehearsal should be stopped, the note went on, for everyone's safety. But Casals and the other musicians decided to finish the final rehearsal of the fourth movement. Afterward, Pablo made a brief speech. "The day will come when our country is once more at peace," he said. "On that day we shall play the Ninth Symphony again." [2] The musicians put away their instruments and prepared to go home. Outside the rehearsal hall, people were building barricades preparing for battle.

Uprisings occurred in Barcelona, Madrid, and other Spanish cities but were, for a time, put down. Before long, however, German Nazis and Italian Fascists began pouring weapons and troops into Spain. They fought in support of General Franco and his military allies, who eventually organized as the Nationalist party. Battles between Spanish Republicans, also called Loyalists, and the forces of Franco's

Nationalists raged across much of Spain.

The Republicans loyal to Spanish democracy were strongest in Catalonia, especially around Barcelona. But as the Spanish Civil War raged on, even the government of Catalonia faltered. German and Italian airplanes bombed Barcelona repeatedly. In retaliation, Spanish citizens calling themselves anarchists attacked anyone suspected of being a Fascist, sometimes executing them without trial. The anarchists burned buildings, seized automobiles, and opened prisons.

In desperation, Casals called on members of Barcelona's Republican government. He implored them to put an end to the violence, but they admitted that they were powerless to do much. "Then you ought to resign,"[3] he said angrily. He then met with leaders of the anarchists and begged them to have a greater respect for the law. "The people are the only law,"[4] he was bluntly told.

On July 12, 1937, Casals directed the Orquestra Pau Casals for the final time. The Barcelona concert raised money to aid victims of the war. Five days later, the sixty-year-old cellist sailed away for a tour of South America. As his sixty-first birthday approached, he performed in many cities in England and the European continent. He did not, however, appear in Germany, despite great demand for him there. He was already strongly opposed to the murderous politics of Nazi dictator Adolf Hitler.

Since autumn 1936, Casals had moved his official residence to the Grand Hotel in Prades, a small French city with a strong Catalan flavor near the Spanish border. He continued making brief visits to Barcelona. There he found ever more destruction, most of it caused by Italian and German war planes. On October 19, 1938, he led his final concert in Spain. At the time, Francisco Franco's soldiers were advancing toward Barcelona. The concert, which included many members of his former orchestra, was held as a benefit for the Children's Aid Society. During a brief trip to San Salvador, Casals found his home filled with pitiful war refugees.

Casals's activities attracted the attention of Francisco Franco's soldiers. General Queipo de Llamo, an aide to Franco, made a radio broadcast and said: "That Pablo Casals! I will tell you what I will do to him if I catch him. I will put an end to his agitation. I will cut off his arms—both of them—at the elbow!"[5] Obviously, it was no longer safe to remain in Spain.

From abroad, Pablo Casals delivered a message of his own. During the intermission of a concert broadcast live on the radio, he delivered a speech in both English and French. He addressed it to the nations of the world. "Do not commit the crime of letting the Spanish Republic be murdered," he pleaded. "If you allow Hitler to win in Spain, you will be the next victims of his madness. The war will spread to all

Europe, to the whole world. Come to the aid of our people!"[6]

Tragically, the nations of the world did not do enough to answer Pablo Casals's plea. In the dead of winter, hundreds of thousands of desperate refugees left Catalonia by crossing the Pyrenees and entering France. Overwhelmed by the human tide, the French government forced most of the outcasts into camps surrounded by barbed-wire fences.

On March 29, 1939, Casals played a concert with the London Symphony Orchestra in London's Royal Albert Hall, another benefit to aid Spanish children. The event was unbearably sad. One day earlier, the city of Madrid, the last Republican stronghold in all of Spain, had fallen to Franco's soldiers.

The Spanish Republic was dead. Casals summed up the tragedy by saying, "The main responsibility for the civil war fell on those who tried to abolish by force a legitimate Government (which had been elected by popular votes a few months before). . . . In all civilized countries one should accept the decision of the people, and those who are not satisfied should wait for the next elections."[7]

Pablo did not have to wander far from the Grand Hotel in Prades to see the misery caused by war. Refugee camps were everywhere. Many had little food and water; some offered no shelter better than holes dug into the frozen ground.

Although his Spanish bank accounts were seized by the

Franco government, Casals was still a wealthy man. He used his French and English accounts to send aid to hundreds of refugees. He rented a large truck, filled it with food and other supplies purchased with his own money, and rode with a driver to nearby camps. There, he did what was possible to aid the starving refugees. "Someone must remember,"[8] he said to anyone willing to listen.

Within a matter of months, his worst fears about the Nazi government of Adolf Hitler were realized. Germany attacked Poland on September 1, 1939. Two days later, France and England declared war on Germany. German soldiers soon conquered Poland and began marching on France. World War II had begun.

Casals knew that he would be murdered if he were captured by either German Nazis or Spanish Fascists. With the Catalan poet Joan Alavedra, he traveled to the French port of Bordeaux. There, he hoped to board a boat, the *Champlain*, scheduled to sail to the United States. Unfortunately, the *Champlain* was bombed and sunk by German airplanes.

Exhausted and hungry, the two men decided to return to Prades. There they found the entrance of the Grand Hotel padlocked. After they banged on the doors, the hotel owner appeared at a window. "The Germans may arrive at any time," the owner said. "And what if they find I've given shelter to Casals? Everyone knows he's an enemy of the Nazis. I have my family to think of."[9]

Fortunately a tobacconist who lived nearby gave the two men shelter. In a few days Casals rented a tiny house and, some months later, a larger one called the Villa Colette. Alavedra and his family moved into the downstairs portion of the Villa Colette. Casals took two tiny rooms upstairs. It was his home for the next nine years.

In November 1942, German soldiers seized control of Prades. The local government was run by Gestapo agents, the dreaded police of the Nazis. "For the first time I lived among men who wore the hated swastika," Casals remembered. "From the moment Hitler had come to power in Germany I had refused to play in that country—the birthplace of Beethoven and Bach which had been so dear to me—but now the Nazis had come to me. We were virtual prisoners of the Germans."[10]

The Villa Colette was watched constantly by Gestapo agents. Casals's two tiny rooms were searched and ransacked several times. Agents warned him that he would be arrested. The people of Prades grew afraid to talk to Pablo when they passed him on the street.

One day three Gestapo officers rode up to the Villa Colette. They found Casals inside. But instead of arresting him, each raised an arm stiffly in the air, the salute of Nazi soldiers and officials. "So you are the Casals our fathers and grandfathers told us about?" one of the Nazis asked.

"I am," Pablo answered.

The officers said that the music of Casals was loved throughout the world. But, of course, they had another question to ask: "And why don't you go and play in Germany?"

"For the same reason I do not go and play in Spain," Pablo answered.

"We think you are mistaken," one of the Nazis said. "Hitler is a great man, who protects artists and the arts."

"That is your opinion; I have mine," Pablo said.

The Nazi soldiers persisted. "Wouldn't you like to come and play in Berlin again? Hitler himself will come and hear you, and if you like we'll put a railway carriage at your disposal."

"No, thank you," Pablo answered. Eventually, the soldiers hinted that they would like Pablo to at least play for them. The cellist insisted that he was not feeling well.

"Just a few notes," one of the men pleaded. Pablo refused.

Finally, the soldiers said that they could not leave without a souvenir. Casals understood that the men needed proof that they had questioned him. The soldiers produced a photograph, and Pablo signed it, writing: "In remembrance of your visit to Prades."

"As they went, and I looked out of the window," Casals recalled of the dangerous visit, "they asked me if they could take a photograph (another proof). I did not see them again. But I had not played for them."[11]

The battles of World War II raged on. Soon, the pitiful

refugees from Spain were joined by millions of others from nations all over Europe. Casals was pained to learn that his old friend and chamber music partner, Alfred Cortot, had played for German soldiers occupying France. Even when the two men met after the war, Casals was barely able to forgive him.

Casals did show that he was capable of forgiveness, however. In 1944, a seventeen-year-old soldier in the Nazi-controlled French army helped save him from arrest. When the war ended, the young man was put on trial for aiding the Germans. Casals saved the young man's life by testifying in court.

Toward the end of 1944, Pablo gave two concerts to raise money for war victims. He ended each with his arrangement of a simple Catalan folk song called *El Cant dels Ocells*, "The Song of the Birds." The melody was created to mimic the sounds birds might have made as they watched the baby Jesus.

In Europe a miracle was already taking place. A huge Allied army landed in France in the summer of 1944. Before long, German soldiers were pulled out of Prades and all of France to protect the fatherland. The nightmare of war was finally ending. As he prepared to pick up the pieces of his life, Pablo Casals was sixty-seven years old.

Chapter 8

CELLIST IN EXILE

The European battles of World War II ended on May 7, 1945, when German officials surrendered to Allied forces.

Several years after the war was over, the young French soldier who had saved Casals from arrest and probable execution came to see him.

"I owe my life to you," the young man said.

But Pablo could only think of the tragic circumstances of the war. "I told him that probably I had only settled a debt, that probably I owed my life to him.

"And so two lives were saved—two lives amid tens of millions lost. How much solace was there in that thought?"[1]

Casals played cello concertos by Robert Schumann and Edward Elgar with the British Broadcasting Company Orchestra at the Royal Albert Hall on June 27, 1945. So many people crowded around the entrance that police had to clear a path for Casals to enter the building. As soon as the concert began, it was obvious that Casals, even at the age of sixty-eight, kept perfect control of his instrument. For an encore, he played Bach's Suite in C Minor for unaccompanied cello.

In a periodical called the *London Philharmonic Post*, Casals wrote a glowing tribute to the British people. He noted that the terrible war had brought about the end of two dictatorial governments, the Nazi government of Germany and the Fascist party of Italy.

"I am sure that history will always preserve the memory of how the British people kept alive the flame of civilisation in wartime," he wrote, "and I am glad that I have lived to see that such things are possible. I was old enough when this war started and I am older still today, but let me say that I have lived fully during these years: I have survived all these great changes throughout the world.

"I have seen the collapse of the two most hateful forms of dictatorship, and having lived through them has given me renewed strength."[2]

Casals gave other concerts and recitals in England. The most notable were with the pianist Gerald Moore. Moore achieved fame by accompanying a number of great virtuosos in chamber music concerts. When he wrote his autobiography, Moore modestly called it, *Am I Too Loud?*

In his book, Moore wrote about the steady stream of people who always seemed to visit Casals in various hotel rooms. Many of the visitors were Spanish Republicans, who, like Casals, were living in exile. Few of the believers in Spanish democracy were willing to live under the dictatorial rule of General Franco.

Casals hoped, and for a time believed, that the end of World War II would bring about the end of Franco's government in Spain. But during the summer and early fall of 1945, his hopes were destroyed. Conversations with exiled Spaniards and European political leaders convinced him that Allied forces were unwilling to remove Franco from power. In a few more years, the United States government provided Franco with hundreds of millions of dollars in economic aid in return for the use of military bases in Spain.

It was almost impossible for Casals to believe that Franco could remain in total control of Spain. "Was it conceivable, I asked myself, that the Spanish people—the very people who had first taken up arms against fascism—were to be doomed to continue living under fascist rule? And the hundreds of thousands of refugees who had believed an Allied victory would mean the return of democracy in Spain—including those who had fought alongside the Allies—were they to be condemned to permanent exile? I recoiled at the thought of such a betrayal, but the evidence mounted on every side."[3]

Shortly before a scheduled recital with Gerald Moore on October 24, 1945, Casals made a terrible decision. While traveling in a car toward Reading, England, the site of the concert, Casals announced to his companions, "I am not going to play after this."[4] As a form of protest to the rule of Francisco Franco, Pablo Casals decided not to play again in public. He agreed to complete concert dates established over the next two weeks. Thereafter, he would perform only in benefit concerts for organizations such as the Red Cross and children's aid societies. He canceled numerous concert and recording contracts. For the same reasons he turned down honorary degrees from England's Oxford and Cambridge universities.

By his seventieth birthday, Casals was living a life of quiet retirement in Prades near the Spanish border. He received birthday greetings from all over the world. Among them were hundreds of cards, letters, and telegrams from Spanish refugees and former members of the Abraham Lincoln Brigade, which had fought alongside Spanish Loyalists during the war. That evening, he listened on the radio to a BBC broadcast dedicated to him. During the live broadcast, fifty cellists played a song he had written in 1927.

People across much of the world asked Casals to reconsider his musical exile. A group of American intellectuals, led by the physicist Albert Einstein, urged him to move to the United States. Casals sent personal replies to everyone who wrote. He thanked them for their concern, but said it was his duty to remain in Prades. For several years, he lived quietly at the Villa Colette. He taught cello to a number of private students and worked on an oratorio, a work for orchestra and singers he called *El Pesebre*, "The Manger."

By 1949 the fortune that Casals had earned during his

performing years was largely gone. He now considered himself poor, but he hardly seemed to mind. He moved from the Villa Colette to a smaller home, actually a gardener's house on a large estate. He named his new home *El Cant dels Ocells*, "The Song of the Birds."

For many years, Casals had been friends with a brilliant Polish pianist named Mieczyslaw Horszowski. Horszowski gave his first public concert at the age of nine. After World War I, Casals and Horszowski had played together often.

Some months before Casals left the Villa Colette, Horszowski had talked in New York City with the well-known violinist Alexander Schneider. Schneider was a member of the famed Budapest String Quartet. As the two men talked, Horszowski suggested the formation of a music festival in little Prades, so that Casals could attend and play. The festival could, Horszowski added, celebrate the two hundredth anniversary of the death of Bach. The proceeds might go to any charity Casals cared to name.

Schneider wrote a letter to Pablo outlining the idea, but the cellist was hesitant. "You cannot continue to condemn your art to complete silence," Schneider wrote back. "If you won't play in public in other countries, then why not let your fellow musicians come from other parts of the world and play with you in Prades? Your protest will remain no less clear."[5] Casals finally agreed.

101

Alexander Schneider traveled to Prades to help Pablo make arrangements for the festival. Before long, some of the most famous performers of classical music in the world also arrived to take part in the concerts. Among them were the pianists Eugene Istomin, Rudolf Serkin, and, of course, Horszowski, the violinists Isaac Stern and Joseph Szigeti, in addition to Schneider. Even earlier, young members of the thirty-piece Bach Festival Orchestra, many of them Americans, also began arriving. Few of them had ever heard Casals play, but they all knew that he was a living legend.

In the summer of 1950, seventy-three-year-old Pablo Casals began conducting rehearsals of the Bach Festival Orchestra in Prades. "I thank you for coming," he said at the first rehearsal. "I love you. And now, let us begin."[6] As always, Casals conducted patiently and with overwhelming concentration. When he stopped the orchestra to explain something he wished changed, he often sang the melody to show how it should be played. The rehearsals continued for three weeks.

"What excitement there was in Prades as the opening day of the festival approached!" Casals remembered. "The whole appearance of the village was transformed—the streets were festooned with banners, streamers and posters, and Catalan flags flew everywhere."[7] In nearby Spain, the Franco government announced that the border across the Pyrenees would be closed to all Spaniards between June 2 and June 20. There were reports, Franco's spokesman said, that Casals and his lieutenant, the violinist Alexander Schneider, were training guerrilla troops for a Communist takeover of the Spanish government.

Despite Franco's efforts, a small group of Spaniards managed to sneak across the border on foot to hear the festival concerts. "That group of Catalans included musicians, professors, workingmen—and one bishop!" Casals recalled. "Some were old friends of mine who had been political prisoners in Spain. One of the group was an elderly shepherd from Spain. 'I brought my sheep with me over the mountain,' he told me."[8]

Over a period of two-and-a-half weeks, twelve concerts were given during the Bach Festival. On June 2, 1950, Casals opened the concert series by performing Bach's Suite in G Major for unaccompanied cello. The final concert ended as he played his arrangement of "The Song of the Birds" for cello and orchestra.

The festival was an enormous success, widely reported in newspapers and magazines throughout the world. A number of recordings were made between the concerts. Some of these old records, and others made at the festival in later years, are still played today on radio stations that feature classical music.

When Horszowski and Schneider first planned it, only a single series of concerts had been considered. But before the

1950 festival was over, a number of virtuosos were already juggling their schedules so that they could attend another the following year. The Bach Festival continued for many years, usually held in Prades. Casals attended for the last time in 1966, when he was nearly ninety years old.

During the second Bach Festival, in 1951, Pablo was introduced to a fourteen-year-old girl named Marta Montañez. Marta was a native of Puerto Rico, where she studied the cello. But she was attending school in the United States. She came to France with her uncle to attend the Bach Festival. Pablo learned that Marta's family were friends of relatives of Doña Pilar.

Marta and her uncle returned to Puerto Rico after the second Bach Festival. Pablo did not see her again for three years. In the meantime, he continued his life in Prades, playing Bach for his own satisfaction, and teaching cello to his private students.

Casals refused to return to Spain. The Franco government grudgingly allowed other Spanish Republicans to return. But Casals refused all offers from friends and musical associates alike to help him go back to his homeland.

In January 1955 an old friend named Francesca de Capdevila died after a long illness. Her last wish was to be buried in Vendrell next to Doña Pilar. Casals returned to Spain briefly for the ceremony. When he visited his magnificent old home in San Salvador, some people believed he had finally returned. But Casals, privately and publicly, had promised never to live in Spain while Franco ruled. He returned to Prades the following day.

Three months past her eighteenth birthday, Marta Montañez returned to Prades with her mother in September 1954. Arrangements had already been made for her to study advanced cello with Casals. Although she was born in Puerto Rico, Marta studied at Marymount School in New York, where she graduated *maxima cum laude*, the school's highest honor.

Like Pablo, Marta was a gifted musician and a great student of languages. Casals, under the tutelage of the Count de Morphy, had learned a half dozen languages himself. Marta was fluent in Spanish, English, French, and Italian, and soon learned Catalan as well. Pablo began calling her Martita, a sign of friendship.

"Of all the pupils I have taught," he said, "Martita was one of the best. . . . I have never had a pupil who learned more rapidly or worked with greater discipline. At the same time, though studying an instrument is of course a serious affair, she brought an irrepressible brightness of spirit to her work. Her gaiety was infectious. I soon discovered that she had a wonderful sense of humor."[9]

After about a year, the old man and the young woman realized that they were in love. From that point on, they were constant companions. Marta didn't worry that Pablo's life seemed to be nearly over while hers was just beginning. In fact, there were great adventures ahead for both of them.

Chapter 9

THE SONG OF THE BIRDS

On December 11, 1955, Pablo and Marta arrived in San Juan, Puerto Rico, aboard the ocean liner *Flandre*. Accompanying them were Pablo's brother, Enrique, and his wife. It was Pablo's first visit to his mother's homeland.

"For me, Puerto Rico was a case of love at first sight!" he said. "Everything my mother had told me about its beauty I now saw with my own eyes. The brilliant sea, the mountains with their opulent flowers and ferns, the massive cloud formations and luminous fields of sugar cane—they simply took my breath away. Above all, I was captivated by the people, by their dignity and gentleness and warmth. And what hospitality! Everywhere, I was greeted with flowers."[1]

For some time, Casals had been receiving letters from many of Puerto Rico's leading citizens urging him to move to the island. In many respects, Puerto Rico and its sunny beaches reminded the old man of his home in Catalonia.

About a week after they arrived, Pablo and Marta traveled to the town of Mayagüez, where Pablo's mother was born more than a century earlier. There, they made an astounding discovery. Marta's mother, Angélica, had been born in the exact same house as Pablo's mother. Although the two births were sixty years apart, they came on the same day of the year, November 13. A brief ceremony was held in which a plaque was unveiled celebrating the birthplace of Doña Pilar. Then the mayor gave a speech, naming Pablo an adopted son of Mayagüez.

Casals was invited to meet the governor of Puerto Rico, Luis Muñoz. The two men talked for some time. The governor talked about his plans to fight poverty and to improve educational and cultural activities on the island. Near the end of the talk, Muñoz made a sudden, and dramatic, appeal. "Don Pablo, join us and live here!" the governor said. "It is the home of your mother. You are already part of our family."[2]

Of course, Pablo was deeply touched by the offer the governor made, which was echoed by many other Puerto Ricans. But he had responsibilities in France and elsewhere, and had to return to Europe. Before he left the island, however, he agreed to direct an ambitious new music program. The *Festival Casals de Puerto Rico*, a series of twelve concerts directed by Casals, was scheduled for the end of April and the beginning of May 1957.

In November 1956, Martita helped Pablo pack up some of his belongings in his little house in Prades. Then they moved to an apartment house overlooking the ocean in San Juan, Puerto Rico. Ouside the door to the apartment, someone placed a little sign that read: *Cant dels Ocells*.

Pablo celebrated his eightieth birthday in San Juan. He also resisted almost continual requests to visit the United States. He was saddened that the United States government chose to support the Spanish government of Francisco Franco. "So long as Franco remains, I must criticize America," he said, "and it is improper for me to accept hospitality from a country I must criticize." He explained that, although he was now living in Puerto Rico, a United States territory, he felt no conflict. Puerto Rico, he said, "is unrepresented in the Congress, has no voice in foreign affairs, and is therefore blameless."[3]

On April 16, 1957, a week before the scheduled opening of the *Festival Casals de Puerto Rico*, Pablo suffered a serious heart attack while conducting a rehearsal. Dr. Paul Dudley White, an American heart specialist who had treated President Dwight Eisenhower after his heart attack, flew to San Juan. For several days, Casals remained in fair condition. Throughout the critical recovery time, he continued talking to people in four different languages.

Leaders of the festival decided to continue with their work as a tribute to Casals. It was agreed that the orchestra would have no conductor. Alexander Schneider led the music from his concertmaster's seat in the violin section. An empty chair, representing the spirit of Casals, was placed on the conductor's podium.

The festival was an enormous success. Among the world-renowned soloists were Isaac Stern and Rudolf Serkin. At the end of the last concert, the orchestra members stood. A recording of Casals performing "The Song of the Birds" was played.

Although many people feared the worst, the severe heart attack left Casals far from dead. He recovered entirely, ready to play the cello and ready for something else. In a simple ceremony in Casals's San Juan apartment, Marta and Pablo were married on August 3, 1957. A religious ceremony was held a short time later. He was eighty years old. She was twenty-one.

"I was aware at the time," Pablo said, "that some people noted a certain discrepancy in our ages—a bridegroom of course is not usually thirty years older than his father-in-law. But Martita and I were not too concerned about what others thought; it was, after all, we who were getting married—not they."[4]

Some people were shocked by the marriage, but England's Queen Elizabeth was not. "How happy I am," she wrote, "knowing dear little Martita, to learn that you are both united."[5] For the rest of Pablo's life, he and his beloved Martita were inseparable.

At an age when most people would retire from active work, Pablo Casals entered one of the busiest periods of his life. During the winter months of 1957-58, he conducted a series of concerts by the newly formed Puerto Rico Symphony Orchestra. At the same time, he accepted the presidency of the Conservatory of Music of Puerto Rico. Both organizations were created under the direction of Festival Casals, Inc. Funding for both was passed by the Puerto Rican legislature.

During this same time, Pablo and Marta had a new home built along the seacoast near the outskirts of San Juan. In the summer the couple traveled back to France, where Pablo continued his work with the Bach Festival in Prades. He kept on making the annual trip for the next seven years.

As if his musical activities were not enough, Casals also turned his attention to his lifelong dream of world peace. With his friend Albert Schweitzer, who had won the Nobel Prize for Peace in 1953, he called for an end to the arms race and a ban on the testing of nuclear bombs. "I hope that the United States and Russia will overlook their political differences in the long-range interests of mankind," he said in a prepared statement. "It is incredible that civilized men can continue to build new and more destructive weapons instead of devoting their energies toward making this a happier and more beautiful world."[6]

Not much later, he was invited to play at a special concert celebrating the thirteenth anniversary of the United Nations. From the General Assembly Hall in the New York headquarters of the United Nations, he played Bach's Sonata No. 2 in D Major for cello and piano. He was accompanied by his old friend Mieczyslaw Horszowski. The concert, which also included other performers, was broadcast to forty-eight different countries around the world.

During the intermission, a recording was played of Pablo making a plea for peace in four different languages. "The anguish of the world caused by the continuation of nuclear danger is increasing every day. . . ." he said in the English version. "How I wish that there could be a tremendous movement of protest in all countries, and especially from the mothers, that would impress those who have the power to prevent this catastrophe."[7]

In the year 1960, Casals took on even more projects. For the first time in thirty-five years, he traveled to California. There, he taught a series of master classes at the University of California at Berkeley. A number of hidden cameras were used to record the historic lessons. The recordings were televised much later on America's Public Broadcasting System.

In July of the same year, he attended for the first time a music festival created by pianist Rudolf Serkin in the little town of Marlboro, Vermont. Although he missed the 1961 Marlboro season because of commitments abroad, he attended quite a few others. He was always a welcome guest in Marlboro, where he gave some memorable performances.

On November 13, 1961, Casals played a concert at the White House for President John Kennedy and guests. At first, he was reluctant to accept the president's invitation. He still opposed United States policy of support for General Franco. But eventually he decided that his appearance might bring attention to the plight of Spain.

At the start of the concert, President Kennedy made a brief introduction. "The work of all artists," the president said, "stands as a symbol of human freedom and no one has enriched that freedom more signally than Pablo Casals."[8] With Mieczyslaw Horszowski and Alexander Schneider, Casals then played music by Mendelssohn, Schumann, and Couperin.

"At the end of the program I interrupted the applause," Casals said. "'Now,' I said, 'I want to play a Catalan folk song.' And I played 'The Song of the Birds,' the theme of the Spanish exiles, to convey what was closest to my heart—freedom for my people. Then I walked to where the President was seated, and we embraced."[9]

In the summer of 1966, a few months before his ninetieth birthday, Casals made his final visit to Prades. Near the end of the festival, a group of people from Vendrell, Pablo's birthplace, came to visit him. Casals greeted them from a second-floor balcony. In a tribute to his music and all of Catalonia, the visitors decided to form a human pyramid. "Perched on one another's shoulders," Pablo said, "with the largest men on the bottom, they raised to the top of the pyramid a small boy who was carrying a goatskin wine bag.

I took the boy in my arms and drank from the wine bag."[10]

Amazingly, the old musician still had a number of fruitful years left in his glorious life. He nearly, but not quite, outlasted the hated rule of General Francisco Franco. Franco died in November 1975, following weeks of nearly comical efforts to keep him alive with elaborate machinery. Political conditions in Catalonia gradually improved. Today, the Catalan flag flies proudly next to the flag of Spain in many public places.

The life of Pablo Casals was perhaps best described by the physicist Albert Einstein. "What I particularly admire in him is the firm stand he had taken," Einstein wrote, "not only against the oppressors of his countrymen, but also against those opportunists who are always ready to compromise with the Devil. He perceives very clearly that the world is in greater peril from those who tolerate or encourage evil than from those who actually commit it."[11]

Pablo Casals 1876-1973

1876 Casals is born in a small Catalan town called Vendrell, about forty-four miles south of Barcelona, Spain. Alexander Graham Bell invents the telephone. Albert Schweitzer, philosopher, medical missionary, and musician, is born. Rutherford B. Hayes is elected president of the U.S.

1877 Queen Victoria of Great Britain is proclaimed empress of India. Thomas Alva Edison invents the phonograph.

1878 David Hughes invents the microphone. Electric street lighting is introduced in London, England.

1879 The Panama Canal Company is organized under Ferdinand de Lesseps. The first electric train is exhibited at the Berlin Trade Exhibition.

1880 James Garfield is elected president of the U.S. Edison and J. W. Swan independently devise the first practical electric lights. Andrew Carnegie develops the first large steel furnace.

1881 Casals hears the cello for the first time. In the U.S. President Garfield is assassinated and is succeeded by Vice President Chester Arthur. The Canadian Pacific Railway is founded.

1882 Edison designs the first hydroelectric plant. Freedom of the press is established in France.

1883 The Metropolitan Opera House in New York City is opened. The first skyscraper is built in Chicago—10 stories. The Orient Express, a train that runs from Paris to Istanbul, Turkey, makes its first trip. The Brooklyn Bridge is opened to traffic.

1884 Grover Cleveland is elected president of the U.S. The first deep tube underground railroad opens in London. Gold is discovered in South Africa.

1885 Queen Maria Cristina becomes regent of Spain. George Eastman manufactures coated photographic paper. The game of golf is introduced to America.

1886 In England Prime Minister William Gladstone introduces a bill for home rule for Ireland. Steam is used to sterilize surgical instruments.

1887 Queen Victoria of Great Britain celebrates her golden jubilee. Emil Berliner improves the phonograph's sound quality. Edison and Swan produce electric lamps. Celluloid film is invented.

1888 Benjamin Harrison is elected president of the U.S. George Eastman perfects the Kodak box camera. John Dunlop invents the pneumatic tire.

1889 Young Pablo Casals is already giving concerts. Cecil Rhodes's British South Africa Company is given a royal charter. Alexandre-Gustave Eiffel designs a 1,056-foot-high tower in Paris.

1890 First motion-picture shows appear in New York. Rubber gloves are used in surgery at Johns Hopkins University, in Baltimore, Maryland, for the first time. The first entirely steel-framed building is erected in Chicago.

1891 Wireless telegraphy is introduced. Construction of the Trans-Siberian railroad in Russia begins. The clothing zipper is invented.

1892 Grover Cleveland is elected president of the U.S. The first automatic telephone switchboard is introduced. Rudolf Diesel patents his internal combustion engine.

1893 Casals, at 16, plays the cello for the Count de Morphy, a friend of Spain's royal family. Hawaii is proclaimed a republic. A World Exhibition is held in Chicago. Karl Benz constructs his four-wheel car. Henry Ford builds his first car.

1894 Casals earns a music scholarship from Queen Maria Cristina of Spain. French Army Captain Alfred Dreyfus is arrested on a treason charge. He is convicted and sent to Devil's Island. A committee is formed to organize modern Olympic Games.

1895 The Casals move to Paris, but before long return to Barcelona. Cuba fights Spain for its independence. Auguste and Louis Lumière invent a motion-picture camera.

1896 William McKinley is elected president of the U.S. Nobel prizes are begun after the death of Alfred Nobel. A hydroelectric plant opens at Niagara Falls. The first modern Olympics are held in Athens.

1897 Casals visits Madrid; he plays with the Madrid Symphony; he later returns to Barcelona to form a string quartet. Queen Victoria celebrates her diamond jubilee.

1898 U.S. declares war on Spain over Cuba. Pierre and Marie Curie discover radium. The first photographs are taken using artificial light.

1899 Casals sets his family up comfortably and travels to Paris and London. The Philippines demand independence from the U.S. Sound receives its first magnetic recording.

1900 British annex Orange Free State and Transvaal in South Africa. The Commonwealth of Australia is created. Human speech is transmitted via radio waves.

1901 Casals goes on American concert tour. U.S. President William McKinley is assassinated; he is succeeded by Theodore Roosevelt. Following a "century of steam," a "century of electricity" begins. Oil drilling begins in Persia (present-day Iran).

1902 Casals returns to Paris. U.S. acquires perpetual control over the Panama Canal. J. M. Bacon becomes the first man to cross the Irish Channel in a balloon.

1903 Casals makes his first phonograph record. The Alaskan frontier is settled. The electrocardiograph is invented. Henry Ford founds the Ford Motor Company. Richard Stieff designs the first teddy bears.

1904 Casals plays at the White House for President Roosevelt. Work begins on the Panama Canal. A company is founded in Berlin for the production of phonograph records.

1905 Casals plays his first series of Russian concerts. Norwegian Parliament decides to separate from Sweden. Albert Einstein formulates his theory of relativity. Rayon yarn is manufactured. The first motor buses run in England.

1906 The word "allergy" is first used in medicine. The San Francisco earthquake kills 700.

1907 New Zealand becomes a dominion within the British Empire. Ivan Pavlov studies conditioned reflexes. Lumière develops a process for color photography. The ship, the *Lusitania*, steams from Ireland to New York in five days.

1908 Robert Taft is elected president of the U.S. The Union of South Africa is established. The General Motors Corporation is established. Fountain pens become popular. Wilbur Wright flies 30 miles in 40 minutes. Ford produces the first Model "T."

1909 Explorer Robert E. Peary reaches the North Pole. The first commercial manufacture of Bakelite inaugurates the Plastic Age.

1910 King Edward VII of England dies and is succeeded by George V. The first deep-sea research expedition is undertaken. The "weekend" becomes popular in the U.S.

1911 The Chinese republic is proclaimed. Charles Kettering develops the first practical self-starter for automobiles.

1914 Casals marries an American singer, Susan Scott Metcalfe. World War I begins. The Panama Canal is opened. Robert H. Goddard begins his rocketry experiments.

1915 The first transcontinental phone call takes place between Alexander Graham Bell in New York and Dr. Thomas A. Watson in San Francisco.

117

1916 Casals plays at the Metropolitan Opera House with Fritz Kreisler and Jan Ignace Paderewski. Woodrow Wilson is reelected president of the U.S. Sir Arthur Eddington investigates the physical properties of stars.

1917 The Trans-Siberian railroad is completed. The first baseball game is played at the Polo Grounds in New York. Russian Revolution overthrows the Czarist system of government.

1918 Casals returns to Paris. President Wilson drafts his Fourteen Points for peace. An armistice is signed between the Allies and Germany on November 11. Harlow Shapley discovers the true dimensions of the Milky Way.

1919 Casals goes to Barcelona where with great difficulty he founds the Orquestra Pau Casals. Wilson presides over the first League of Nations meeting in Paris. Babe Ruth hits a 587-foot home run for the Boston Red Sox.

1920 The Casals orchestra gives its first concert. The U.S. Senate votes against joining the League of Nations. Guglielmo Marconi opens the first public broadcasting station—in Berlin. The Eighteenth Amendment for prohibition is passed in the U.S.

1921 Warren Harding becomes president of the U.S. The tuberculosis vaccine is developed. The first radio broadcast of a baseball game is made from the Polo Grounds in New York.

1922 The League of Nations approves mandates for Palestine and Egypt. In India, Mohandas K. Gandhi is sentenced to 6 years' imprisonment for civil disobedience. Benito Mussolini of Italy forms a Fascist government. The new Ku Klux Klan gains popularity in the U.S.

1923 An Argentinean swimmer, Enrique Tiroboschi, swims the English Channel in 16 hours. Colonel Jacob Schick invents the electric razor.

1924 Calvin Coolidge is elected president of the U.S. Insecticides are used for the first time. Pioneer work is done in electrocardiography.

1925 Adolf Hitler reorganizes the Nazi party and publishes volume 1 of *Mein Kampf*. Inventor John Baird transmits recognizable human features by television. The Charleston becomes a fashionable dance.

1926 Casals gives his first Workingman's Concert. Queen Elizabeth II of England is born. Germany is admitted to the League of Nations. Lord Halifax is named viceroy of England. Roald Amundsen and Lincoln Ellsworth fly over the North Pole in an airplane.

1927 "Black Friday" in Germany—the economic system collapses. Al Jolson makes *The Jazz Singer*, the first talking motion picture. Charles Lindbergh flies the *Spirit of St. Louis*. The Harlem Globetrotters basketball team is organized. Babe Ruth hits 60 home runs for the New York Yankees.

1928 Women's suffrage in Britain is reduced from the age of 30 to 21. Herbert Hoover is elected president of the U.S. Alexander Fleming discovers penicillin. Teleprinters and teletypewriters come into restricted use in the U.S., Britain, and Germany.

1929 Arabs attack Jews in Palestine following disputes over Jewish use of the Wailing Wall. The U.S. Stock Exchange collapses. Byrd and three companions fly over the South Pole. Six notorious gangsters are killed in Chicago in the St. Valentine's Day Massacre.

1930 British White Paper on Palestine suggests that British immigration be halted. In the German election Nazis gain 107 seats from the center parties. The British Broadcasting Corporation Symphony Orchestra is founded. Photoflash bulbs come into use. Karl Lansteiner wins the Nobel Prize for medicine for grouping of human blood.

1931 King Alfonso XIII is forced to flee from Spain; Casals conducts a joyful concert. The Matterhorn in the Alps is climbed for the first time. The George Washington Bridge between New Jersey and New York is opened.

1932 Franklin D. Roosevelt is elected president of the U.S. Auguste Picard reaches a height of 17.5 miles in his stratosphere balloon. Amelia Earhart is the first woman to fly across the Atlantic.

1933 Hitler is appointed chancellor of Germany; political parties, other than the Nazis, are suppressed. Approximately 60,000 artists (authors, actors, painters, musicians) emigrate from Germany.

1934 Casals meets Albert Schweitzer in Scotland. Oswald Moseley introduces Fascist mass meetings in Britain. Hitler and Mussolini meet in Venice. German plebescite votes for Hitler as führer. Winston Churchill warns British Parliament of German air menace.

1935 President Roosevelt signs the U.S. Social Security Act. Pierre and Marie Curie receive the Nobel Prize for chemistry for the synthesis of new radioactive elements.

1936 Franco is forced into exile; Spanish Civil War begins. King George V of England dies; he is succeeded by his son Edward VIII. Gossip begins in London about King Edward VIII's relationship with Mrs. Wallis Simpson; he abdicates and is succeeded by his brother, George VI. Mussolini and Hitler proclaim the Rome-Berlin Axis.

1937 Casals directs the Orquestra Pau Casals for the final time. Germany and Italy support Franco's forces. George VI is crowned king of Great Britain. The Royal Commission on Palestine recommends the establishment of Arab and Jewish states.

1938 Germany mobilizes. Neville Chamberlain, prime minister of Great Britain, meets Hitler. Churchill leads public outcry at British appeasement. Roosevelt recalls U.S. ambassador to Germany. Gas masks are issued to British citizens.

1939 Casals plays a concert in London's Royal Albert Hall for the benefit of Spanish children. Spain falls to Franco, ending the civil war. Germany concludes nonaggression pact with U.S.S.R. and alliance with Italy. Germany invades Poland and annexes Danzig. Great Britain and France declare war on Germany. Roosevelt declares U.S. neutral.

1940 Germany invades Norway and Denmark. Churchill makes his "blood, sweat, and tears" speech. Heavy air raids on London. U.S. passes Selective Service Act to mobilize the military. Roosevelt elected president of the U.S. for third term. Penicillin is developed as a practical antibiotic.

1941 Germany invades the Soviet Union. Churchill and Roosevelt meet and sign Atlantic Charter. Royal Air Force bombs Nuremburg, Germany. Japanese bomb Pearl Harbor. U.S. and Britain declare war on Japan. Germany and Italy declare war on U.S. U.S. declares war on Germany and Italy.

1942 U.S. transfers more than 100,000 Japanese-Americans to West coast internment camps. Germans reach Stalingrad. The murder of millions of Jews in gas chambers begins. Gandhi demands independence for India and is arrested.

1943 New German attacks on London. Allied forces in North Africa are placed under General Dwight D. Eisenhower's command. U.S. forces regain islands in Pacific from Japanese. Churchill, Roosevelt, and Stalin hold Teheran conference. Allied "round-the-clock" bombing of Germany begins.

1944 Heavy air raids on London. D-day: Allies land on Normandy, France. Charles de Gaulle enters Paris. U.S. troops land in Philippines. Franklin Roosevelt elected for fourth term. Vietnam declares herself independent of France.

1945 As a protest Casals decides not to play again in public until Franco's dictatorship in Spain ends. Roosevelt dies; Harry S. Truman becomes president of the U.S. Mussolini is killed by Italian partisans. Hitler commits suicide. Berlin surrenders to Russians and Germany capitulates. "V.E. Day" ends war in Europe. Churchill, Truman, and Stalin confer at Potsdam, Germany. U.S. drops atomic bombs on Hiroshima and Nagasaki in Japan. Japan surrenders.

1946 U.N. General Assembly holds its first session, in London. Churchill gives his "Iron Curtain" speech. Albania, Bulgaria, Yugoslavia, and Czechoslovakia adopt Communist governments.

1947 British proposal to divide Palestine is rejected by Arabs and Jews. Question is referred to U.N., which announces plan for partition. India is proclaimed independent and is partitioned into India and Pakistan.

1948 In India, Gandhi is assassinated. Churchill chairs Hague conference for European unity. The Jewish state of Israel comes into existence. Arab armies attack Israel. Truman is elected president of the U.S.

1949 China falls to the Communists. Communist People's Republic is proclaimed under Mao Tse-tung. Israel is admitted to U.N. Israel signs cease-fire agreements with Jordan, Syria, Egypt, and Lebanon. German Federal Republic (West Germany) and German Democratic Republic (East Germany) come into being. Apartheid is established in South Africa.

1950 Casals agrees to conduct rehearsals for the Bach Festival Orchestra in Prades, organized by Alexander Schneider and a number of famous musicians. Britain recognizes Communist China. Truman instructs Atomic Energy Commission to develop hydrogen bomb. North Korean forces invade South Korea, beginning the Korean War. Senator Joseph McCarthy begins his "witch hunt" for Communists and subversives in America.

1951 J. Andre-Thomas devises a heart-lung machine for heart operations.

1952 Anti-British riots erupt in Egypt. King George VI of England dies; he is succeeded by his daughter Queen Elizabeth II. Churchill announces that Britain has produced an atomic bomb. Dwight Eisenhower is elected president of the U.S.

1953 Jonas Salk begins inoculating children with polio vaccine. Concern rises in Europe and America about fallout from radioactive waste. The Korean War ends.

1954 Colonel Gamal Abdel Nasser seizes power in Egypt. U.S. Supreme Court rules that segregation by color in public schools is unconstitutional. Vietnam is divided.

1955 South Vietnam becomes a republic.

1956 Sudan proclaimed independent democratic republic. Suez War; Jordan and Israel accept U.N. truce proposals. Nasser elected president of Egypt. Nasser seizes Suez Canal; British and French nationals leave Egypt. Fidel Castro lands in Cuba intent on overthrow of Fulgencio Batista.

1957 Casals and Marta are married. The Casals Festival begins in Puerto Rico. Casals becomes president of the Conservatory of Music of Puerto Rico. Israeli forces withdraw from Sinai Peninsula and hand over Gaza Strip. U.N. reopens Suez Canal to navigation. U.S.S.R. launches *Sputnik I* and *II*, the first earth satellites. Vietnam war develops.

1958 The European Common Market comes into being. Castro begins "total war" against the Batista government in Cuba. U.S. launches first moon rocket.

1959 Castro becomes premier of Cuba. The first nuclear-powered submarine, the *Savannah*, is launched. The Soviet Union launches rocket with two monkeys aboard.

1960 Casals teaches master classes at the University of California at Berkeley. John F. Kennedy is elected president of the U.S. The American Heart Association associates higher death rate from heart attacks with smoking of cigarettes.

1961 Casals plays for President Kennedy and guests at the White House. Queen Elizabeth tours India, Pakistan, Persia, Cyprus, and Ghana. The Berlin Wall is constructed. British Prime Minister Edward Heath begins negotiations for British entry into Common Market. Alan Shepard makes first U.S. space flight.

1962 U.S. military council established in South Vietnam. Soviet Union agrees to send arms to Cuba.

Kennedy announces establishment of Soviet missile base in Cuba. Under pressure it is finally dismantled.

1963 U.S. and U.S.S.R. agree to "hot line" from White House to the Kremlin. President Kennedy assassinated; Lyndon B. Johnson becomes president of U.S. President of South Vietnam assassinated. The Beatles become a popular singing group.

1964 Reverend Martin Luther King, Jr., leader of the civil-rights movement, wins the Nobel Peace Prize. Winston Churchill makes his last appearance in the House of Commons shortly before his 90th birthday. *Ranger VII*, launched from Cape Kennedy, returns close-up photographs of the moon's surface. U.S. begins bombing of North Vietnam.

1965 Winston Churchill dies. There are outbreaks of violence in Selma, Alabama. Martin Luther King, Jr. leads 4,000 civil-rights demonstrators in march from Selma to Montgomery. U.S. marines are sent to Vietnam.

1966 Casals makes his final visit to Prades. Mrs. Indira Gandhi becomes prime minister of India. Michael deBakey plants arteries leading to an artificial heart, which function through a three-and-a-half-hour valve-replacement operation.

1967 Six-day war between Israel and Arab nations. Israeli forces move into Sinai Desert and Jordan, capture old city of Jerusalem, and gain control of Sinai approaches to Suez Canal. In the U.S., 50,000 persons demonstrate against the Vietnam War. Dr. Christiaan Barnard performs first human heart-transplant operation.

1968 Reverend Martin Luther King, Jr. is assassinated. Student rioting begins in Paris. De Gaulle returns to Paris. U.S. spacecraft lands successfully on the moon. Senator Robert F. Kennedy is assassinated. Richard Nixon is elected president of the U.S.

1969 Hundreds of Americans demonstrate against the Vietnam War. *Apollo II* lands on moon's surface; Neil Armstrong sets down on it and takes a walk.

1970 U.S. student protests against Vietnam War result in killing of 4 by National Guard at Kent State in Ohio. Almost 500 colleges and universities are closed or on strike. Nuclear-powered heart pacemakers are successfully implanted in three patients.

1971 Violence worsens in Northern Ireland after Britain institutes policies of preventive detention and internment without trial. U.S. bombs Vietcong supply routes in Cambodia and conducts large-scale bombing raids against North Vietnam.

1972 Richard Nixon is reelected president in a near-record landslide. District of Columbia police arrest 5 men inside Democratic National Headquarters in the Watergate Hotel, beginning the "Watergate Affair." Ireland, Britain, and Denmark agree to full participation in the European Economic Community.

1973 Pablo Casals dies on October 22. Fighting breaks out in the Middle East between the Arabs and the Israelis. After initial gains the Arabs are pushed back. Arab oil-producing nations move to embargo shipments to the U.S. The cutoff precipitates an energy crisis in the industrialized world.

NOTES

Chapter 1
1. Randall Peffer, "Catalonia: Spain's Country Within a Country," *National Geographic* (January 1984): 106
2. Pablo Casals, as told to Albert E. Kahn, *Joys and Sorrows* (New York: Simon & Schuster, 1970): 18
3. J. Ma. Corredor, *Conversations with Casals*, translated from the French by Andre Mangeot (New York: E. P. Dutton & Co., Inc., 1958): 15
4. Ibid., 16
5. Casals, *Joys and Sorrows*, 31
6. Ibid., 29-30
7. H. L. Kirk, *Pablo Casals* (New York: Holt, Rinehart and Winston, 1974):33
8. Casals, *Joys and Sorrows*, 32
9. Ibid., 33-34
10. Ibid., 34

Chapter 2
1. H. L. Kirk, *Pablo Casals*, 39
2. Pablo Casals, *Joys and Sorrows*, 35
3. Ibid.
4. Ibid., 36
5. J. Ma. Corredor, *Conversations with Casals*, 22
6. Ibid., 25
7. Ibid., 24
8. Casals, *Joys and Sorrows*, 40-41
9. Ibid., 41
10. Kirk, *Pablo Casals*, 52
11. Casals, *Joys and Sorrows*, 42
12. Ibid.

Chapter 3
1. Pablo Casals, *Joys and Sorrows*, 47
2. Ibid., 48
3. J. Ma. Corredor, *Conversations with Casals*, 27
4. H. L. Kirk, *Pablo Casals*, 67
5. Casals, *Joys and Sorrows*, 58
6. Ibid., 60
7. Kirk, *Pablo Casals*, 87
8. Casals, *Joys and Sorrows*, 66

9. Lillian Littlehales, *Pablo Casals* (New York: W.W. Norton & Company, 1929; revised and enlarged 1948): 30-31
10. Casals, *Joys and Sorrows*, 70

Chapter 4
1. Pablo Casals, *Joys and Sorrows*, 70-71
2. J. Ma. Corredor, *Conversations with Casals*, 37
3. Casals, *Joys and Sorrows*, 77
4. Ibid.
5. H. L. Kirk, *Pablo Casals*, 108
6. Casals, *Joys and Sorrows*, 144
7. Ibid., 145
8. Corredor, *Conversations with Casals*, 40-41
9. Casals, *Joys and Sorrows*, 93

Chapter 5
1. Pablo Casals, *Joys and Sorrows*, 101
2. Ibid., 102-03
3. J. Ma. Corredor, *Conversations with Casals*, 51
4. Casals, *Joys and Sorrows*, 104
5. Corredor, *Conversations with Casals*, 51
6. Ibid.
7. Casals, *Joys and Sorrows*, 110
8. Lillian Littlehales, *Pablo Casals*, 57-58
9. Casals, *Joys and Sorrows*, 135-36

Chapter 6
1. H. L. Kirk, *Pablo Casals*, 299
2. Pablo Casals, *Joys and Sorrows*, 142
3. Ibid., 146
4. J. Ma. Corredor, *Conversations with Casals*, 70
5. Casals, *Joys and Sorrows*, 154
6. Corredor, *Conversations with Casals*, 71
7. Lillian Littlehales, *Pablo Casals*, 96
8. Casals, *Joys and Sorrows*, 158
9. Kirk, *Pablo Casals*, 336
10. Casals, *Joys and Sorrows*, 165

Chapter 7
1. Pablo Casals, *Joys and Sorrows*, 218-19
2. Ibid., 219

3. H. L. Kirk, *Pablo Casals*, 402
4. Ibid.
5. Casals, *Joys and Sorrows*, 226
6. Ibid., 227
7. J. Ma. Corredor, *Conversations with Casals*, 214
8. Kirk, *Pablo Casals*, 410
9. Casals, *Joys and Sorrows*, 238
10. Ibid., 241
11. Corredor, *Conversations with Casals*, 216-17

Chapter 8
1. Pablo Casals, *Joys and Sorrows*, 248
2. H. L. Kirk, *Pablo Casals*, 426-27
3. Casals, *Joys and Sorrows*, 256
4. Kirk, *Pablo Casals*, 433
5. Casals, *Joys and Sorrows*, 261-62

6. Kirk, *Pablo Casals*, 454
7. Casals, *Joys and Sorrows*, 262
8. Ibid., 264
9. Ibid., 269

Chapter 9
1. Pablo Casals, *Joys and Sorrows*, 271-72
2. Ibid., 272
3. H. L. Kirk, *Pablo Casals*, 490-91
4. Casals, *Joys and Sorrows*, 277
5. Kirk, *Pablo Casals*, 499
6. Casals, *Joys and Sorrows*, 284
7. Kirk, *Pablo Casals*, 507
8. Ibid., 520-21
9. Casals, *Joys and Sorrows*, 290
10. Ibid., 266
11. J. Ma. Corredor, *Conversations with Casals*, 11

INDEX - *Page numbers in boldface type indicate illustrations.*

About the Author

Jim Hargrove has worked as a writer and editor for more than ten years. After serving as an editorial director for three Chicago area publishers, he began a career as an independent writer, preparing a series of books for children. He has contributed to works by nearly twenty different publishers. His Childrens Press titles include biographies of Mark Twain, Daniel Boone, Thomas Jefferson, Lyndon B. Johnson, Steven Spielberg, Diego Rivera, Nelson Mandela, and Richard Nixon. With his wife and daughter, he lives in a small Illinois town near the Wisconsin border.